THE

GORGEOUS

KITCHEN

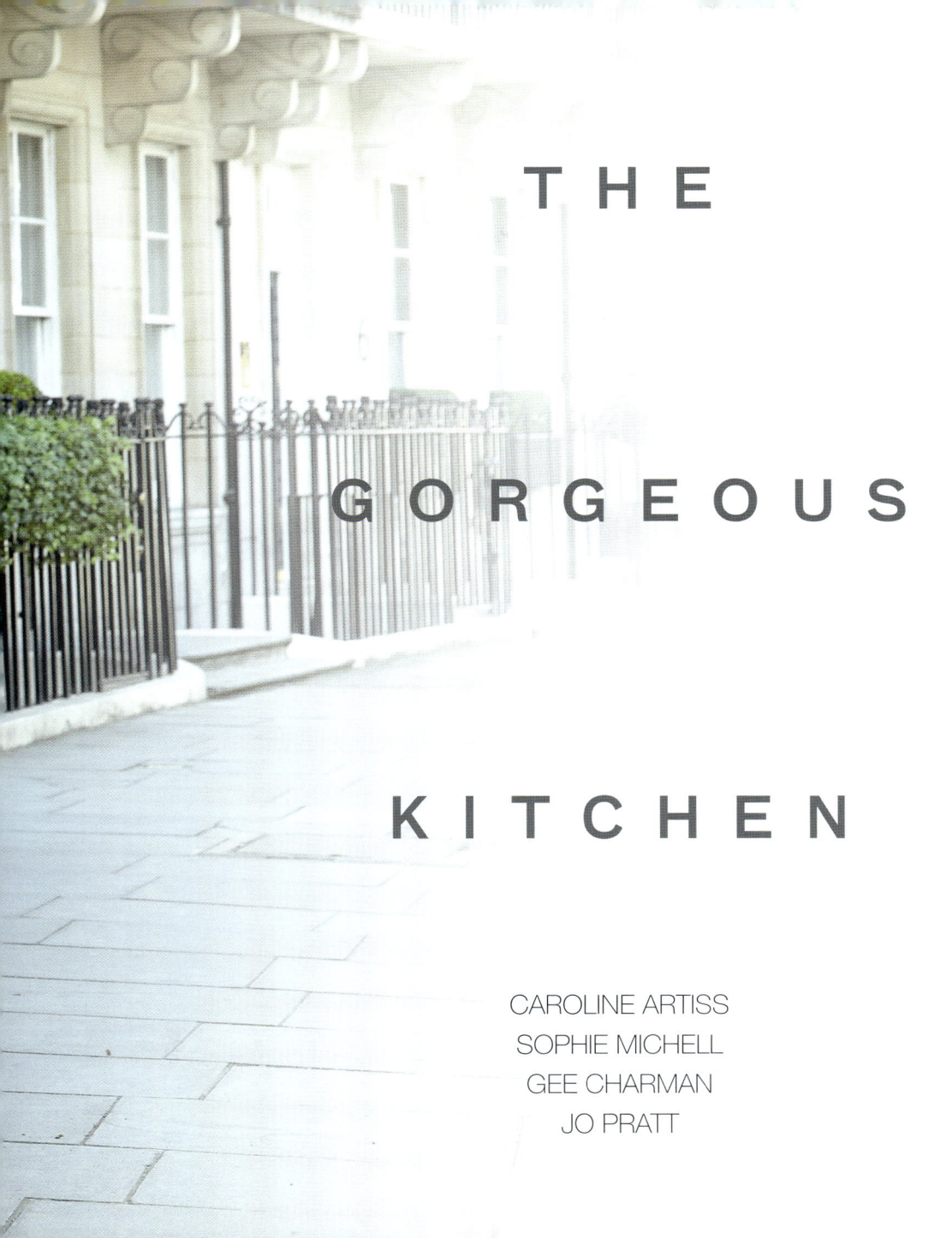

THE

GORGEOUS

KITCHEN

CAROLINE ARTISS
SOPHIE MICHELL
GEE CHARMAN
JO PRATT

CONTENTS

FOREWORD

At Autogrill/HMSHost we wanted to bring something extra special to The Queen's Terminal – the new Terminal 2 at London's Heathrow airport. So we created and designed The Gorgeous Kitchen restaurant, working in collaboration with four brilliant female British chefs. The restaurant is a fusion of style, design and great food with fast and friendly service, catering to the needs of passengers day and night, as they travel through the airport and beyond.

At our restaurant, which has fabulous views of the planes and runway, we aim to bring you a great British dining experience set within the magnificent environment of one of the world's busiest airports. Fresh, seasonal produce is lovingly prepared by people who are as passionate about food as you are.

In creating this book, the chefs have lent their expertise, experience and personalities to create over eighty unique recipes. These are recipes you can use from breakfast to dinner, for everyday or special occasions, as well as a few cheeky cocktail ideas for those summer parties!

The recipes are designed to celebrate beautiful, simple but full-flavoured ingredients – gorgeous dishes that will be a wonderful reminder of your visit to The Gorgeous Kitchen in London Heathrow's Terminal 2.

CAROLINE ARTISS

"Always so positive, Caroline's phenomenal enthusiasm has kept us all fired up – The Gorgeous Kitchen will be trending worldwide thanks to her creative energy!"

I trained as a chef when I was 15, and have now worked in the food world for over 20 years. As a single mum with next to nothing, I launched a YouTube cooking show, which now teaches many thousands of people around the world how to cook simple, delicious meals! The show was picked up by TV, and since then I've cooked my way across the USA for BBC's America's *Chef Race* and filmed my own series for Malaysian TV called *Simply Caroline*. I've really loved working with the others to put together this, my first cookery book, and I can't wait for the next adventure!

SOPHIE MICHELL

"It's been thrilling to work with such a talented and creative chef. Sophie's influence has been invaluable in helping craft the perfect menu."

I have been cooking in kitchens since I was 15 and recently became executive chef at Belgraves Hotel in London, making me the youngest female executive chef in the UK. Prior to this I have worked in well-known London restaurants and I was also private chef to Claudia Schiffer for two years. All this, plus my love of travelling, has influenced my recipes for The Gorgeous Kitchen. It's been brilliant working with the girls on The Gorgeous Kitchen and this is my fifth cookery book.

JO PRATT

"So lovely to work with, the gorgeousness of this book is very much down to Jo's natural flare for making food look beautiful."

Having published five cookery books and worked with many great chefs, I'm thrilled to get the chance to launch a restaurant with the other gorgeous girls. I think everyone should be able to cook great food at home, and I hope the recipes in this book will help you to do just that. I have previously been the food editor for *Elle* and *Glamour* magazines but, despite working with so many fantastic people, my husband and children are still my harshest food critics!

GEE CHARMAN

"We love Gee's can-do attitude and she's always up for a laugh – working with her on launching the restaurant has been so much fun!"

I've been so lucky in my career, working everywhere from palaces to prisons! I started off as a private chef for The Duke and Duchess of Gloucester at Kensington Palace, where curtsying was the order of the day. However, my knees wore out so I decided to venture into private catering where I could design menus based around individual tastes and needs. A chance encounter led me into the world of TV where I now help top chefs from around the world make their food come alive on screen as well as in their books. This is my first restaurant venture and I can't wait!

BREAKFAST

SMOKED SALMON ON PUMPERNICKEL TOAST WITH LEMON CRÈME FRAÎCHE, DILL AND PUMPKIN SEEDS

Smoked salmon, dill and lemon is a classic food combination made in heaven. This luxurious but simple breakfast is also delicious on classic soft rye or granary toast.

Preparation time: 5 minutes
Cooking time: 5 minutes

SERVES 4

INGREDIENTS

100g (3½oz) crème fraîche
zest of 1 lemon, plus a few squeezes of juice
sea salt and freshly ground black pepper
1 tbsp unsalted butter
2 tbsp pumpkin seeds
4 slices of pumpernickel bread
200g (7oz) sliced smoked salmon
a few dill fronds, to serve

1 Mix together the crème fraîche, lemon zest and juice and season, to taste, with salt and pepper.

2 Heat the butter in a frying pan over a low to medium heat, then stir in the pumpkin seeds. Toast the seeds in the butter for a couple of minutes until they start to pop, then sprinkle with salt. Remove from the pan and drain on kitchen paper.

3 Toast the pumpernickel bread, then spread with some of the crème fraîche mixture. Top with slices of smoked salmon, a sprinkling of toasted seeds and, finally, scatter with the dill and serve.

TROPICAL SUPER JUICE

Bring a burst of sunshine to your day! After a glass of this juice, you'll be full of get-up-and-go thanks to the energy-giving properties of the fruits and the super-hydrating coconut water. The enzymes from the pineapple are great for your digestion, and will maximize the extraction of all of the other nutrients in the drink, giving a huge boost to your energy levels.

Preparation time: 10 minutes

MAKES 2 LARGE GLASSES

INGREDIENTS

2 passion fruits, halved
1 ripe mango, peeled and chopped
½ small pineapple, peeled and cut into
   chunks
12 fresh lychees, peeled and de-stoned
   (use tinned if fresh not available)
juice of ½ lime
375ml (13fl oz) coconut water, chilled

1 Scoop out the pulp from the passion fruits into a blender – strain it through a sieve if you don't want the seeds.

2 Add the remaining ingredients and blitz until you have a smooth consistency. Pour into glasses and enjoy straightaway.

Tip

For an extra energy boost, throw a peeled banana into the blender too.

"If you're a new convert to juices in the morning, Jo's Tropical Super Juice is perfect. Sunshine in a glass, that will get you up and awake!"

GRIDDLED PINEAPPLE WITH PASSION FRUIT AND MINT

This is a great alternative to a classic fruit salad: it's sweet and tangy all at the same time. Caramelizing the pineapple on a griddle adds warmth and brings out the flavour of even an under-ripe fruit.

Preparation time: 10 minutes
Cooking time: 10 minutes

SERVES 4

INGREDIENTS

1 small pineapple
2 tbsp golden caster sugar, plus 1 tsp
20 mint leaves
2 passion fruits
juice of 1 lime

1 With a sharp knife, slice the top and bottom off the pineapple, then cut off the skin. Halve the fruit down the middle, and then cut each half into 4 to give you 8 long wedges. Carefully cut out and discard the core from each wedge. Heat a griddle pan over a high heat.

2 Dust the pineapple wedges with 1 tablespoon of sugar, then place them on the hot griddle. Cook for about 3 minutes on each side, so lovely charred lines appear.

3 While the pineapple is cooking, crush 1 tablespoon of the sugar and the mint leaves in a pestle and mortar until you have a bright green sugar.

4 Scoop out the pulp from the passion fruit into a small saucepan. Add the 1 teaspoon of sugar and the lime juice. Bring to a simmer over a low heat for a minute or so, stirring occasionally until the sugar has dissolved. Remove from the heat.

5 Serve the griddled pineapple with some of the passion fruit dressing spooned over the top and sprinkled with the mint sugar.

MATCHA, CRANBERRY AND ORANGE BREAKFAST MUFFINS

These freshly baked muffins are jam-packed full of 'good for you' ingredients, so don't feel guilty about having more than one! The Matcha green tea powder not only adds a subtle yet distinctive flavour and a fabulous colour but it also provides a huge dose of antioxidants that will definitely jump-start your day.

Preparation time: 10 minutes
Cooking time: 20 minutes

MAKES 12 MUFFINS

INGREDIENTS

175g (6oz) wholemeal self-raising flour
4½ tsp Matcha green tea powder
2 tsp baking powder
40g (1½ oz) porridge oats
110g (4oz) soft brown sugar
75g (3oz) dried cranberries
2 tbsp linseed
3 tbsp pumpkin or sunflower seeds
finely grated zest of 1 large orange
4 tbsp rapeseed or sunflower oil
2 large eggs
240ml (8fl oz/1 cup) low-fat natural yoghurt

1 Heat the oven to 190°C (375°F/gas 5). Line a 12-cup muffin tray with muffin cases.

2 Stir together the flour, Matcha powder, baking powder, three-quarters of the oats, the sugar, cranberries, linseed and pumpkin or sunflower seeds until well combined.

3 In a separate bowl or jug, mix together the orange zest, oil, eggs and yoghurt. Pour on to the dry ingredients and mix until just combined.

4 Spoon the mixture into the muffin cases and scatter the remaining oats over the top.

5 Bake for 20 minutes or until the muffins have risen and are cracking slightly on top. Remove from the oven and cool slightly before eating warm or at room temperature.

Tip

If the muffins don't get eaten on the day of baking, store in an airtight container for up to a couple of days. You can also freeze the muffins, and then defrost them overnight before heating through at a low temperature.

BLUEBERRY FRENCH TOAST

I'm a big fan of French toast for a weekend brunch, because it's so easy and tasty. This recipe is a sweeter version, which is why I like to use brioche. Teamed with the sweet blueberries and tart Greek yoghurt, it's a perfect combination of flavours.

Preparation time: 5 minutes
Cooking time: 10 minutes

SERVES 2

INGREDIENTS
3 eggs
120ml (4fl oz) milk
1 tbsp caster sugar
½ tsp cinnamon
2 thick slices of brioche
butter, for frying

For the blueberry compote
200g (7oz) blueberries
1 tbsp sugar

To serve
Greek yoghurt
honey, agave syrup or maple syrup
fresh mint

1 Start by making the blueberry compote. It's really easy: just heat the blueberries, sugar and 1 tablespoon of water in a small pan over a medium heat for 2–3 minutes, until the blueberries have exploded a bit and they have started to turn a bit mushy. Remove from the heat and leave to cool.

2 Meanwhile, whisk the eggs, milk, sugar and cinnamon together in a large bowl. Heat a large frying pan over a medium heat. Dunk the brioche slices in the egg mixture, soaking both sides. Add a little butter to your heated pan, then place the soaked brioche in the pan and cook for 1–2 minutes on each side, until golden brown and the egg is cooked through. Don't have the heat too high as the brioche might burn before cooking through.

3 Serve the French toast hot, straight from the pan, with dollop of Greek yogurt, a spoonful of your blueberry compote, a drizzle of something sweet and a sprig of mint. Only one word: YUM!!!

QUINOA 'PORRIDGE' WITH GOJI BERRIES, ALMOND MILK AND CINNAMON

This was suggested to me by my head chef, Dominic Taylor, at my restaurant, Pont St. Quinoa has become very fashionable over the past few years, but even I was sceptical about using it to make porridge. It turns out that it tastes lovely! The cinnamon and vanilla make it taste sweet and the amino acids, proteins and antioxidants from the quinoa and goji berries mean it's very good for you too. It's also dairy free.

Preparation time: 5 minutes
Cooking time: 5 minutes

SERVES 4

INGREDIENTS

300g (10½oz/1²/₃ cups) cooked quinoa
400ml (13fl oz) almond milk
2 tbsp ground almonds
2 tbsp goji berries
1 tsp ground cinnamon
½ tsp vanilla extract
4 tbsp agave syrup
2 tbsp flaked almonds

1 Very simply, put the quinoa, almond milk, ground almonds, goji berries, cinnamon, vanilla and agave syrup in a saucepan, bring to a simmer and warm through.

2 Meanwhile, dry-fry the almond flakes in a small pan until lightly golden, and sprinkle on top of each serving.

"A fantastic and healthy way to start your day, especially before travelling. Wheat free, dairy free and it will keep you full for ages."

FLUFFY COCONUT AND LIME PANCAKES WITH PASSION FRUIT CURD AND YOGHURT

Everyone loves pancakes, and here is my fresh take on a classic. These wonderfully fluffy pancakes zing from a touch of lime, and the passion fruit curd is packed full of flavour. I love making curds from all sorts of fruit – they keep for a week in the fridge and I dollop them on everything from crumpets and toast to ice cream.

Preparation time: 10 minutes, plus 30 minutes resting

Cooking time: 40 minutes

INGREDIENTS

75g (2½oz/¾ cup) desiccated coconut
200g (7oz/1⅔ cups) self-raising flour
10g (⅓oz) baking powder
2 tbsp caster sugar
1 tsp salt
1 egg
100g (3½oz) butter, melted (warm not hot!)
1 tsp vanilla extract
375ml (12fl oz) milk
1 tsp lime zest

For the passion fruit curd

8 passion fruits
100g (3½oz/½ cup) caster sugar
2 eggs, plus 2 egg yolks
juice of 1 lime
25g (1oz) unsalted butter

To serve

200ml (7fl oz) Greek yoghurt
1 lime, cut into wedges

1. To make the passion fruit curd, halve the passion fruits and scoop the flesh and seeds into a saucepan. Add the sugar, eggs, egg yolks and lime juice and whisk o combine. Set the saucepan over a medium heat and stir continuously for 10 minutes, until the egg mixture thickens and coats the back of the spoon – take great care not to let the mixture boil or bubble, as it will split. When the curd is thick and creamy, remove from the heat, whisk in the butter and leave to cool.

2. Toast the desiccated coconut in a dry pan for a couple of minutes, until golden. Set aside 2 tablespoons to garnish the pancakes and tip the rest into a large mixing bowl. Add the rest of the pancake ingredients and whisk to make a batter. Leave to rest for 30 minutes. Preheat the oven to 140°C (275°F/gas 1).

3. Heat a non-stick frying pan over a medium heat. Spoon a ladle of batter into the pan, cook for about 4 minutes, until small bubbles start to appear on the surface, then flip over and cook the other side for a couple of minutes. Depending on the size of your pan, you should be able to cook 2 at a time. Keep warm in a low oven while you cook the remaining pancakes.

4. Serve the pancakes with the Greek yoghurt, passion fruit curd, a sprinkling of coconut and a wedge of lime.

HERBY EGG WHITE OMELETTE WITH RAW ENERGY SALSA

This is true energy food, which won't make you feel tired nor bloated – WIN WIN! The raw salsa is full of pure, lovely, delicious nutrients so, if you can, make it just before you need it so the ingredients don't lose any of their fantastic goodness.

Preparation time: 15 minutes
Cooking time: 5 minutes

SERVES 2

INGREDIENTS

6 egg whites
2 tbsp chopped mixed herbs (a mixture of
    coriander/cilantro, basil and chives)
a pinch of celery salt
olive or rapeseed oil, for frying
optional: 1–2 tbsp finely grated
    Parmesan cheese

For the salsa

¼ small red onion, peeled and finely diced
¼ red (bell) pepper, finely diced
¼ green (bell) pepper, finely diced
1 large ripe tomato, de-seeded and finely diced
½ ripe avocado, peeled, de-stoned and
    finely diced
1 tsp finely diced green chilli
juice of ½ lime
1 tbsp avocado or rapeseed oil
salt and pepper

1 Mix together the salsa ingredients in a small bowl. Season, to taste, with salt and pepper and set aside.

2 Using a balloon whisk, lightly whisk half the egg whites with half the herbs and a good pinch of celery salt.

3 Heat a trickle of oil in a small non-stick frying pan over a medium heat. Pour in the herby egg whites and stir them continuously using the underside of a fork (be careful not to scratch the pan), until the eggs are starting to set like scrambled egg. Leave to continue cooking until the whites are cooked through and not runny. Scatter over the Parmesan, if using.

4 Carefully fold the omelette over, transfer to a plate and serve with the salsa. Repeat to make the second omelette.

Tip

If you're not sure what to do with the egg yolks, there are endless ways to use them up: Hollandaise sauce, mayonnaise, pasta carbonara, quiche, custard, ice cream, crème brûlée, chocolate pots . . . even a DIY face mask (the yolks contain loads of vitamin A).

GREEN EGGS WITH SPINACH, AVOCADO AND PESTO

I first had green eggs on a work trip to California – they have the most bountiful supply of avocados out there. The freshness of the pesto really brightens up the dish and eating this for breakfast or brunch always starts my day in a good way.

Preparation time: 10 minutes
Cooking time: 5 minutes

INGREDIENTS

2 big handfuls of baby spinach
2 chunky slices of sourdough
4 eggs
1 tbsp white wine vinegar
1 ripe Hass avocado, peeled, de-stoned
    and sliced
salt and pepper

For the pesto
a big handful of fresh basil
2 tbsp toasted pine nuts
1 garlic clove, peeled
1 tbsp grated Parmesan or pecorino cheese
a pinch of coarse sea salt
zest of ½ lemon
4 tbsp olive oil

1   First make your pesto by simply putting all the ingredients in a blender and whizzing until smooth. Leave to one side.

2   Fill a large shallow pan with water to a depth of about 7.5cm (3in) and bring to the boil. Dunk the spinach in the water and leave for 15 seconds, then remove with a slotted spoon and place in a sieve. Sprinkle some cold water over the top and then set aside. Keep the water in the pan simmering over a medium heat – you can use it to poach your eggs.

3   Get your bread toasting while you cook the eggs. Add the vinegar to the pan of simmering water and then carefully crack the eggs into individual cups. Slide them, one at a time, into the water. Once the water has returned to a simmer, poach the eggs for about 3 minutes (more if you like the yolks firm). Lift out the eggs with a slotted spoon and use some kitchen paper to drain off the excess water from underneath the spoon.

4   While the eggs are cooking, squeeze any excess water from the spinach and place a small mound on each piece of toast. Top with the avocado slices. Place the eggs on top of the avocado and drizzle with a few blobs of pesto. If the pesto is too thick, add a bit more oil. Season with a pinch of salt and some pepper. If you like, you can serve the toast on the side to avoid getting soggy bread!

Tip

Fresh is always best, but when you're short on time – or basil – use a good-quality ready-made pesto instead. If you have any fresh pesto left over you can freeze it, or cover it with a little olive oil and keep it in the fridge for up to a week.

BUBBLE AND SQUEAK CAKES
WITH POACHED EGGS AND CRISPY BACON

I often have these for brunch the morning after a night out as . . . ahem . . . a hangover cure. You can also try them with black pudding, sausages, large roast mushrooms or grilled tomatoes – but whatever ingredients you go for, you definitely need a good dollop of delicious TGK onion marmalade on the side! You'll find the recipe on page 105.

Preparation time: 30 minutes
Cooking time: 30 minutes

SERVES 4

INGREDIENTS

1kg (2lb 4oz) Maris Piper potatoes, peeled
   and quartered
40g (1½ oz) butter
2 onions, peeled and sliced
500g (1lb 2oz) cooked cabbage or
   Brussels sprouts, roughly chopped
2 tsp Dijon mustard
salt and pepper
50g (2oz) plain (all-purpose) flour
olive oil, for shallow frying
12 slices of streaky bacon, smoked
   or unsmoked
1 tbsp white wine vinegar
4 eggs
TGK onion marmalade, to serve
   (see page 105)

1 Steam the potatoes over a large pan of boiling water for 15–20 minutes until tender. Once cooked, drain and mash well.

2 Meanwhile, melt the butter in a frying pan and cook the onions until softened and turning golden brown.

3 Mix together the mashed potatoes, onion, cooked cabbage or sprouts and mustard. Season well with salt and pepper. Shape into 4 small or 8 larger rounds and dust each one with flour.

4 Pour the oil into a large frying pan to a depth of about 5mm (¼in). Heat the oil over a medium heat and fry the cakes for 2 minutes on each side, until golden brown. If your pan isn't big enough to cook them all at the same time, you can keep the cakes warm in a low oven while you cook the rest.

5 While you are cooking the cakes, grill the bacon, or fry it in a trickle of oil in a separate pan, until crisp.

6 Add the vinegar to a medium-sized saucepan of water and bring to a simmer over a medium heat. Crack the eggs into individual cups, and then slide one egg at a time into the water. Once the water has returned to a simmer, poach the eggs for 3 minutes (more if you like the yolks firm). Lift the eggs out with a slotted spoon and sit them on kitchen paper to drain off the excess water.

7 Once everything is cooked, serve the bubble and squeak cakes topped with the poached eggs and bacon. Spoon some onion marmalade on to the side and serve immediately.

Tip

Traditional British bubble and squeak is made with leftover vegetables from a roast dinner, so you can use carrots, peas or whatever veg you have.

SALADS & SOUPS

GORGONZOLA, GRILLED NECTARINE AND RADICCHIO SALAD

After spending years in the Med, I am always inspired by simple ingredients put together to make luxurious dishes. In this recipe, the sweet char-grilled juicy nectarine really works well with the spicy, strong blue cheese, and the Marcona almonds provide a perfect buttery crunch.

Preparation time: 10 minutes
Cooking time: 5 minutes

SERVES 4

INGREDIENTS

2 nectarines, halved, stone removed and
    each half cut into quarters
100g (3½oz) Marcona almonds
a bunch of watercress
2 heads of radicchio, trimmed and
    leaves separated
300g (10½oz) Gorgonzola
    Piccante, crumbled

For the dressing

1 tbsp white balsamic vinegar
100ml (3½fl oz) extra virgin olive oil
1 tsp honey
sea salt and pepper

1 Heat a griddle pan over a high heat and cook the nectarines for about 2 minutes on each side, until char lines appear.

2 Meanwhile, lightly toast the almonds in dry pan for a few minutes to bring out their flavour and colour. Pick off and discard some of the thicker stems from the watercress.

3 To make the dressing, whisk together all ingredients. Place the watercress and radicchio in a bowl and lightly dress the leaves, to taste.

4 Arrange the cheese, nectarine pieces and salad leaves on serving plates and scatter over the almonds.

ROAST SQUASH, FETA AND QUINOA SALAD WITH FRESH HERBS AND TOASTED HAZELNUTS

This has to be one of my favourite salads as it has everything in it – you don't need to make anything else to go alongside. Serve it in a giant bowl, put it in the middle of your table and watch it magically disappear. It's also a good idea to have some copies of the recipe to give out – you'll need them.

Preparation time: 25 minutes
Cooking time: 40–50 minutes

SERVES 4

INGREDIENTS

1 medium butternut squash, peeled and
   cut into bite-sized pieces
3 red onions, peeled and cut into wedges
3 tbsp olive oil
salt and pepper
60g (2½oz) hazelnuts
50g (2oz/¼ cup) quinoa
1 radicchio or 50g (2oz) ruby chard,
   roughly chopped
a small bunch of mint leaves, roughly chopped
a small bunch of flat-leaf parsley leaves,
   roughly chopped
½ small bunch of chives, roughly chopped
1 red chilli, de-seeded and finely chopped
400g (14oz) barrel-aged feta cheese, crumbled

For the dressing

2 tbsp rapeseed oil
2 tbsp hazelnut oil
2 tbsp honey
1 tbsp white wine vinegar
1 tbsp wholegrain mustard
finely grated zest of ½ orange

1 Preheat the oven to 200°C (400°F/gas 6). Place the butternut squash and onions in a roasting tray and toss in the oil. Season with salt and pepper then roast for 40–50 minutes, until softened and starting to turn golden. Once cooked, remove from the oven and leave to cool to room temperature.

2 While the vegetables are cooking, spread the hazelnuts over a small baking tray and roast in the oven for 8 minutes, until golden. Remove from the oven, allow to cool, then crush them on a board with the flat edge of a large knife. Set aside.

3 To cook the quinoa, rinse well in cold water, then put in a saucepan with twice its volume of cold water. Add a pinch of salt, bring to the boil over a high heat, then cover with a tight-fitting lid and reduce the heat to low. Cook for 12 minutes then turn off the heat and, without removing the lid, leave for a further 5 minutes.

4 To make the dressing, place all the ingredients in a jar with a lid and give it a good shake.

5 To finish the salad, gently toss the squash, onions, quinoa, radicchio or chard, herbs, chilli and feta together in a large bowl with the dressing. Scatter over the hazelnuts and serve.

Tip

All the salad ingredients can be prepared a good few hours in advance or even the day before – keep them in the fridge but make sure you bring the squash and onions back to room temperature before serving. Assemble and mix with the dressing right at the last minute.

KING PRAWN, SHAVED FENNEL AND AVOCADO SALAD WITH PINK GRAPEFRUIT DRESSING

This is a great alternative to a classic fruit salad: it's sweet and tangy all at the same time. Caramelizing the pineapple on a griddle adds warmth and brings out the flavour of even an under-ripe fruit.

Preparation time: 10 minutes

SERVES 4

INGREDIENTS

1 pink grapefruit
2 Little Gem lettuces, leaves separated
100g (3½oz) watercress
1 avocado, stone removed and cut
   into wedges
1 fennel bulb, very thinly sliced using
   a mandolin
400g (14oz) cooked king prawns

For the dressing

1 egg yolk
50ml (2fl oz) light olive oil
salt and pepper

1 Segment the grapefruit by slicing the peel off using a sharp knife and cutting the flesh into segments. Reserve any juice that is on your cutting board and pour into a bowl.

2 To make the dressing, whisk the egg yolk until light and fluffy, then gradually add the oil in a slow trickle. Be careful not to add too much in one go. Keep whisking while adding the reserved grapefruit juice and then season, to taste.

3 To assemble the salad, arrange the lettuce, watercress, avocado, grapefruit segments and fennel on individual plates or on one large platter. Top with the prawns and drizzle over the dressing.

VIETNAMESE CHICKEN AND
GREEN MANGO SALAD

This salad reminds me of being back in Asia eating a blow-your-head-off spicy, yet very refreshing salad. You don't have to make it as spicy as this – I'll leave that up to you – but I think it is a great combination of flavours and textures in a mouth- (and sometimes eye-) watering salad.

Preparation time: 15 minutes
Cooking time: 15–20 minutes

SERVES 4

INGREDIENTS

2 skinless chicken breasts
1 tsp sesame oil
pepper
2 under-ripe, green mangos, peeled and
  cut into long, thin strips
1 large carrot, peeled and chopped
  into matchsticks
½ cucumber, halved lengthways, de-
  seeded and chopped into matchsticks
½ small red onion, peeled, sliced into very
  thin rings and soaked briefly in cold water
2 tbsp freshly chopped Thai sweet basil
  leaves (or regular will do)
2 tbsp freshly chopped mint leaves
2 tbsp roasted peanuts, roughly chopped
2 tbsp crispy fried shallots (see page 47)

For the dressing

juice of 2 limes
3 tbsp palm sugar, or 1½ tbsp caster sugar
  and 1½ tbsp light brown sugar
2 garlic cloves, peeled and finely minced
2 tbsp fish sauce
1 bird's eye chilli (or 2 if you like spicy!)
1 tbsp dried shrimps, finely chopped
  (you can find these in your local Asian
  food shop)

1 Start by cooking the chicken breasts. Preheat the oven to 180°C (350°F/gas 4). Rub a dash of sesame oil and a pinch of pepper all over the chicken, then wrap in foil and pop in the oven for 15–20 minutes, depending on how big they are. Once cooked, remove from the foil and leave to cool. Use your fingers to shred the meat.

2 Place the mango strips in a large bowl with the carrot, cucumber, onion and chicken.

3 Mix together all the ingredients for the dressing in a small bowl until the sugar has dissolved.

4 Pour the dressing over the salad and give it a good stir. Sprinkle the chopped herbs over the top and toss through. Heap the salad on to plates, scatter over the chopped peanuts and crispy shallots and serve immediately.

Tip

Use a serrated vegetable peeler or a mandolin with a julienne attachment to slice the mango.

ROASTED SALMON, NEW POTATO AND PEA SHOOT SALAD WITH A SHALLOT AND CAPER DRESSING

Summer is the time to eat well and get adventurous with salads. Forget the simple cucumber, lettuce and tomato combo and give this a go. To make a change from salmon, try grilled artichoke hearts or chicken.

Preparation time: 25 minutes
Cooking time: 25 minutes

SERVES 4

INGREDIENTS

4 x 200g (7oz) salmon fillets, skin on
salt and pepper
90ml (3fl oz) olive oil, plus 1 tbsp
450g (1lb) baby new potatoes
150g (5oz) green beans
2 banana shallots, peeled
1 tbsp honey
1 tbsp Dijon mustard
2 tbsp sauvignon blanc vinegar
1 tbsp capers in vinegar, drained
75g (2½oz) frozen peas, defrosted
100g (3½oz) pea shoots

1 Preheat the oven to 180°C (350°F/gas 4). Place the salmon in a roasting dish, skin-side up, and season with salt and pepper. Drizzle over the 1 tablespoon of oil. Cook in the oven for 15–20 minutes, or until the fish is firm to the touch.

2 While the fish is cooking, boil the potatoes in a large pan of salted water for 8–10 minutes, until tender. With the pan still on the heat, use a slotted spoon to remove the potatoes and set aside to cool. Add the beans to the hot water and cook for 1 minute. Drain and refresh under cold running water or plunge into a bowl of iced water.

3 Finely dice half a shallot and finely slice the remaining one and a half. Set aside the diced shallot. Place the sliced shallot in a bowl, season with a little salt, then pour over enough boiling water to cover it. Leave for 5 minutes and then drain.

4 Whisk together the honey, mustard and vinegar. Slowly whisk in the 90ml (3fl oz) oil. Once all the oil has been added, whisk in 1 teaspoon of warm water – this will help emulsify the dressing. Add the diced shallots to the dressing along with the capers then season, to taste, with salt and pepper – you can always add a little more vinegar or honey if you like.

5 Remove the salmon from the oven and carefully peel off the skins. Preheat the grill to high. Place the skins on a wire rack, sprinkle with salt, then pop them under the hot grill for 3–4 minutes, until golden brown and crisp.

6 Place the potatoes in a bowl along with the beans and peas. Dress with half the dressing and divide between 4 serving plates. Scatter over the pea shoots, then break up each salmon fillet into large chunks and add to the salad. Drizzle with the remaining dressing then top with shards of the crispy skin for added texture.

THAI BEEF NOODLE SALAD

If you're after something healthy, filling and delicious, then this is the salad for you. Many of the ingredients are raw or only very briefly blanched, so they won't have lost any of their nutrients by being cooked for too long. Use your favourite steak; I like to use rump or sirloin – or fillet, if I'm feeling flash!

Preparation time: 25 minutes, plus marinating time
Cooking time: 10 minutes

INGREDIENTS

400g (14oz) steak
100g (3½oz) green beans
100g (3½oz) baby corn
300–400g (14oz) fine rice noodles
2 large handfuls of bean sprouts
2 carrots, peeled and cut into matchsticks
½ cucumber, de-seeded and finely sliced
   into long thin strips (use a mandolin or
   vegetable peeler)
2 tbsp freshly chopped coriander (cilantro)
2 tbsp freshly chopped Thai sweet basil
   (or regular will do)
peanut or vegetable oil, for frying

For the marinade
1 tbsp cumin
1 tbsp ground coriander (cilantro)
1 tsp turmeric
2 tsp Chinese Five Spice powder
salt and pepper

For the dressing
½ tbsp sesame oil
2 tbsp soy sauce
3 tbsp sweet chilli sauce
1 tbsp finely chopped fresh ginger
2 garlic cloves, peeled and finely chopped
2 red Thai bird's eye chillies, finely chopped
   (or more if you like it hot!)
2 tsp fish sauce
juice of 2 limes

1 Mix together all the spices for the marinade in a bowl. Rub them all over the steak and leave to marinate for a couple of hours – but don't worry if you don't have that much time, 30 minutes will be fine.

2 Meanwhile, bring a saucepan of water to the boil and blanch the green beans and baby corn for 1 minute. Drain and refresh under cold running water or in a bowl of iced water. Slice the baby corn in half lengthways.

3 If you are using dried noodles, simply pour hot water over them and let them soak according to the packet instructions. If you have fresh ones, pour hot water over them and leave them for a few seconds. Run them under cold water and drain in a colander.

4 When your steak has finished marinating, mix together all the ingredients for the dressing. Transfer the noodles to a bowl. Pour over just under half of the dressing and mix through.

5 In a separate bowl, combine all of the vegetables. Mix through some more of the dressing, reserving a couple of tablespoons for serving.

6 Pile the noodles on to a serving platter and scatter over the vegetables and most of the chopped herbs – save some for garnishing at the end.

7 Now all you have to do is cook your steak! Heat a frying pan or griddle pan until hot, then brush with a little oil. Cook the steaks for 2–3 minutes on each side – longer if you like your steak well done or if they are particularly thick.

8 When your steak is cooked to your liking, rest it on a board for a few minutes, then slice and scatter it on top of the salad. Drizzle over the rest of the dressing and serve.

WARM SPICED LAMB, AUBERGINE AND CHICKPEA SALAD

This recipe is bursting with flavour, not only from the aromatic spices coating the lamb and aubergine, but also from the tangy and herby sesame dressing. I sometimes like to add some fried avocado on top too, which adds a surprising smoky flavour to the dish, not dissimilar to the taste of bacon.

Preparation time: 20 minutes
Cooking time: 15–20 minutes

SERVES 4

INGREDIENTS

1 tsp ground cumin
1 tsp ground coriander (cilantro)
½ tsp hot chilli powder
4 tbsp olive oil
salt
1 medium aubergine (eggplant), sliced into
    rounds 5mm (¼in) thick
4 x 110g (4oz) lamb leg steaks
350g (12oz) cooked chickpeas
    (drained weight)
1 red onion, peeled and finely sliced
4–6 ripe tomatoes (depending on their
    size), quartered
2 handfuls of de-stoned black
    Kalamata olives
a bunch of mint leaves, roughly chopped
a bunch of flat-leaf parsley leaves,
    roughly chopped

For the dressing

2 tbsp tahini
2 tbsp lemon juice
2 tbsp finely chopped fresh oregano
6 tbsp extra virgin olive oil
salt and pepper

1   Mix the cumin, coriander, chilli powder and 3 tablespoons of the olive oil in a large bowl. Season with salt and then add the aubergine and lamb. Mix well to coat in the spiced oil then leave for about 10 minutes for the flavours to soak in.

2   Meanwhile, make the dressing by simply mixing everything together and seasoning with salt and pepper.

3   Heat a large frying pan over a high heat until hot and then fry the lamb steaks for 2–3 minutes on each side. Transfer them to a plate to rest while you cook the aubergine.

4   Add the aubergine to the pan in a single layer (you may need to cook it in batches if your pan isn't large enough) and fry for 2–3 minutes on each side until soft and golden. Remove from the pan and set aside (on the same plate as the lamb).

5   Keeping the pan on the heat, add the remaining tablespoon of oil and fry the chickpeas for 2 minutes, until they are heated through and have started to take on the odd bit of colour. Transfer to a large bowl.

6   Add the onion, tomatoes, olives, mint and parsley to the bowl. Toss in half of the dressing and divide between serving plates.

7   Sit the aubergine on top. Slice the rested lamb and place on top of the aubergine. Finish by drizzling over the remaining dressing and any resting juices from the lamb.

Tip

If lamb isn't your thing, try swapping it for chicken breast, beef fillet or even some sliced halloumi.

CHILLED WATERMELON AND RED PEPPER SOUP WITH FETA AND PUMPKIN SEED 'CROÛTONS'

This refreshing soup is great at any time of the year but particularly when it's wonderfully hot and sunny. The soup is delicious on its own, but take it to a new level by serving it with the salty, tangy and lightly spiced 'croûtons'.

Preparation time: 15 minutes, plus 2 hours to chill

Cooking time: 30 minutes

SERVES 4

INGREDIENTS

2 red (bell) peppers

600g (1lb 5oz) watermelon flesh, cut into chunks and seeds removed (from approx. 1kg/2lb 4oz wedge)

½ red chilli, de-seeded and roughly chopped

1 small garlic clove, peeled and crushed

2 tsp pomegranate molasses

8 large mint leaves

salt and pepper

extra virgin olive oil, for drizzling

For the 'croûtons'

110g (4oz) feta cheese

50g (2oz/⅓cup) pumpkin seeds

1 tbsp olive oil

¼ tsp dried chilli flakes

½ tsp sumac

1 Heat the grill to high and grill the peppers for 15–20 minutes, turning occasionally, until they are charred all over. Put them in a plastic sandwich bag and seal, or place them in a bowl and cover with cling film. Leave the peppers for about 10 minutes until they are cool enough to handle, then peel away and discard the skins and seeds.

2 Place the grilled peppers in a food processor or blender with the watermelon, chilli, garlic, pomegranate molasses and mint leaves. Season with salt and pepper. Blitz well until you have a very smooth soup. Place in the fridge for at least 2 hours until totally chilled.

3 To prepare the 'croûtons', heat the oven to 220°C (425°F/gas 7). Break the feta into small chunks and gently mix together with the pumpkin seeds, oil, chilli flakes and sumac.

4 Spread the mixture in a single layer on a non-stick baking tray and bake for 10–12 minutes, turning once. When cooked, the feta should be starting to turn golden in places and the pumpkin seeds will be crunchy and puffed up. Serve either warm or at room temperature scattered over the soup. Drizzle the soup with a little oil just before serving.

Tip

Don't be put off by having to grill your own peppers – they take hardly any time at all. However, if you're really stretched for time, buy a jar of peppers that are already grilled.

HOMEMADE TOMATO SOUP

This is one of my daughter's favourite lunches on a cold winter day. She likes to eat her soup with grilled cheese sandwiches to dunk in. I do, too, so have included the recipe for my grilled-cheese-with-a-kick-sandwich. Alternatively, serve it with crusty wholemeal bread.

Preparation time: 10 minutes
Cooking time: 50 minutes

SERVES 4

INGREDIENTS

2 x 400g (13fl oz) tins of whole plum tomatoes
1–2 tbsp olive oil
1 tsp freshly chopped thyme
2 tbsp butter
1 small onion, peeled and diced
2 garlic cloves, peeled and roughly chopped
1 tbsp tomato purée
750ml (24fl oz) vegetable stock
1 tsp caster sugar
2 tbsp basil leaves
2 tbsp double (heavy) cream
salt and pepper

1 Preheat the oven to 200°C (400°F/gas 6). Drain the juice from the tomatoes into a bowl and keep to one side. Arrange the tomatoes on a baking tray, drizzle with oil, scatter over the thyme and cook in the oven for 30 minutes.

2 About 5 minutes before the tomatoes are going to be ready, melt the butter in a large saucepan over a low heat. Add the onion and garlic and leave to soften for 5 minutes. Stir in the roasted tomatoes, the tomato purée, vegetable stock and reserved tomato juice. Simmer for a further 20 minutes.

3 Turn off the heat, stir in the sugar, basil and cream, and season with a good pinch of salt and pepper. Blitz until smooth, then check the seasoning and serve with some lovely crusty bread, or the grilled cheese sandwiches, below.

GRILLED CHEESE AND JALAPEÑO SANDWICHES

Preparation time: 5 minutes
Cooking time: 5 minutes

SERVES 1

INGREDIENTS

butter
2 thick slices of soft white bread
2 slices of Gruyère (or Cheddar) cheese
   (1 slice should cover a piece of bread)
a few chunky slices of pickled jalapeños

1 Heat a heavy-based frying pan over a low to medium heat. Generously butter one side of both pieces of bread all the way to the edges. Place the cheese slices and jalapeños on one of the unbuttered sides. Top with the other piece of bread, buttered bread on the outside.

2 Place the sandwich in the pan and cook for 2 minutes on each side, until golden brown all over and the cheese is melted. The trick here is to cook it slowly so you don't burn the bread.

BUTTERNUT SQUASH, KAFFIR LIME LEAF AND COCONUT SOUP

Thailand is at the top of my 'must-visit' list. I love how they season their food, perfectly balancing their dishes with a mixture of salt, sweet, hot, bitter and sour flavours – this soup captures them all in one bowl.

Preparation time: 15 minutes
Cooking time: 20 minutes

SERVES 4

INGREDIENTS

2 tbsp light olive oil, plus extra to serve
2 garlic cloves, peeled and sliced
1 mild to medium heat red chilli, finely
    diced (remove the seeds if you don't want
    it too hot)
750g (1lb 7oz) butternut squash, peeled
    and cut into 1cm (½in) dice
250ml (8fl oz) vegetable stock
400g (14oz) tin of coconut milk
5 Kaffir lime leaves
3 tbsp fish sauce
fresh coriander (cilantro) leaves, to serve
toasted coconut strips, to serve

1   Heat the oil in a large saucepan over a medium heat. Add the garlic and most of the chilli, reserving a little for a garnish. Fry for 1 minute and then add the butternut squash. Cook, stirring occasionally, until the edges of the squash start to soften, then pour in the stock and coconut milk.

2   Scrunch up the Kaffir lime leaves to help release their oils, then add them to the pan. Stir to combine, then cover with a lid, reduce the heat and simmer for about 10 minutes, until the squash is tender.

3   When the squash is cooked, transfer everything to a blender and blitz until smooth. Pour the soup back into the hot pan and season with the fish sauce.

4   Serve in deep bowls drizzled with a few drops of oil and scattered with the reserved chopped chilli, the coriander leaves and a few strips of toasted coconut.

CLASSIC CHICKEN BROTH WITH SHELLED BEANS, PEAS AND HERBS

I always have a chicken broth of some sort on my menus. Chicken broth is a dish that everyone craves now and again, and it really does restore your body and spirit – a bowl of comforting chicken broth will have you feeling right in minutes. This one has extra aromatic herbs and some spring veggies for good measure.

Preparation time: 20 minutes
Cooking time: 3 hours 20 minutes

INGREDIENTS

For the stock

1 free-range or organic chicken, washed
   inside and out
2 carrots, roughly chopped
2 onions, peeled and roughly chopped
3 garlic cloves, peeled and roughly chopped
1 parsnip, roughly chopped
2 leeks, roughly chopped
3 sticks of celery, roughly chopped
a few bay leaves
a bunch of flat-leaf parsley
a bunch of dill
a bunch of tarragon
a sprig of fresh thyme

For the soup

2 carrots, peeled and cut into 1cm (½in) dice
2 leeks, cut into 1cm (½in) dice
1 celeriac, peeled and cut into 1cm (½in) dice
salt and pepper
100g (3½oz) peeled broad beans
150g (5oz) peas
1 tbsp freshly chopped flat-leaf parsley

1. Place the chicken in a large saucepan, add all the veggies and then cover with water. Add the herbs and bring to the boil. Turn down the heat and simmer gently, then skim any scum off the surface and continue to simmer for about 3 hours.

2. When the stock is tasting good, strain all the liquid into another large saucepan. Discard the veg but reserve the chicken. Pick the meat off the chicken and set aside.

3. Add the chopped vegetables for the soup to the stock, bring to the boil and simmer for 20 minutes. While the soup is simmering, shred the chicken. Season the soup with salt and pepper and add the chicken, beans, peas and parsley. Warm through briefly and serve.

PRAWN RAMEN WITH SPRING ONIONS AND CORIANDER

This is a beautifully light but filling meal. The warming stock and noodles make a perfect contrast to the fresh red onions, coriander and fiery chilli. It's perfect for when you are feeling under the weather or off on a long journey.

Preparation time: 15 minutes
Cooking time: 20 minutes

SERVES 4

INGREDIENTS

16 shell-on raw king prawns
3 tbsp sweet chilli sauce
1 tbsp white wine, malt or rice wine vinegar
1 tbsp caster sugar
2 tbsp fish sauce, plus extra to taste
1l (32fl oz) light chicken or vegetable stock
400g (1lb) ramen noodles
½ small red onion, peeled and finely sliced
4 spring onions (scallions), finely sliced
a small bunch of coriander (cilantro), roughly chopped
1 red chilli, finely chopped (remove the seeds if you don't want it too hot)
1 lime, cut into wedges

1 Peel and de-vein the prawns, leaving on the very end of the tail and reserving the heads and shells. Set aside.

2 In a saucepan placed over a medium heat, mix together the sweet chilli sauce, vinegar and sugar and warm through until the sugar has dissolved. Once it has started to bubble, add the fish sauce, stock and the reserved prawn shells and heads. Bring to the boil and simmer gently for 5 minutes, then strain the stock into a clean saucepan.

3 Place the stock over a medium heat and bring to a simmer. Add the prawns to the stock and simmer gently for 4 minutes or until the prawns are firm to the touch and a lovely pink colour. Season with extra fish sauce.

4 Meanwhile, bring a pan of salted water to the boil. Add the noodles, cook for 4 minutes and then drain.

5 Divide the drained noodles between 4 deep bowls and pour the stock and prawns over the top. Scatter over the sliced red onion, spring onions, chopped coriander and chilli, and serve with a wedge of lime.

LIGHT BITES

SEA BASS AND SCALLOP CEVICHE WITH CRISPY SHALLOTS

I'm a huge fan of all types of ceviche but my recipe has a bit of an Asian twist to it, as I add some freshly grated ginger. You can eat the ceviche just as it is because it's so flavoursome, but I like to serve it on top of a tortilla chip or tostada with a spoonful of guacamole and a sprinkle of crispy fried shallots. Delish!

Preparation time: 15 minutes, plus 1 hour to chill

Cooking time: 10 minutes

SERVES 4–6

INGREDIENTS

150g (5oz) sea bass, cut into very small cubes
150g (5oz) scallops, cut into very small cubes
140ml (5fl oz) freshly squeezed lime juice
1 heaped tbsp freshly grated ginger
2 tbsp finely diced or sliced red onion
1½ tbsp freshly chopped coriander (cilantro)
1 tbsp freshly chopped flat-leaf parsley
a big pinch of caster sugar
1 serrano chilli, de-seeded and finely chopped
½ tsp each of salt and freshly ground
   black pepper

For the crispy shallots

375ml (12fl oz) sunflower or canola oil
2 large shallots, peeled and finely sliced
1 tbsp cornflour
salt and white pepper

To serve

ripe avocado or guacamole
optional: tortilla chips or tostadas

1   Place the cubed sea bass and scallops in a non-reactive bowl and pour the lime juice over the top. Add the ginger, cover the bowl with cling film and leave in the fridge for 1 hour. The fish 'cooks' in the acid of the lime juice and it will turn white and opaque.

2   Meanwhile, make the crispy fried shallots. Pour the oil into a wok or frying pan set over a low to medium heat. Separate the slices of shallot and press a piece of kitchen paper on top of them to remove as much moisture as possible. Spread them out on your chopping board and use your fingertips to coat the shallots in the cornflour.

3   To test whether the oil is hot enough, drop in one piece of shallot. It should sizzle when it touches the oil and turn brown in about 30 seconds. If it's not hot enough, the shallots won't be crispy and will end up soggy. Cook the shallots, a handful at a time, for 1–2 minutes, or until golden brown. Do not over-crowd the pan. Using a slotted spoon transfer the shallots to a piece of kitchen paper, spread them out and leave to drain. Keep them spread out until they have cooled down, then sprinkle with a pinch each of salt and white pepper and set aside in a bowl. (They are best eaten and used on the same day, but you can keep them in an airtight container for a few days if they are crispy enough!)

4   When the ceviche is ready, drain off most of the lime juice and then add all the other ingredients. Give it a good stir and serve immediately with the crispy shallots and some avocado, and tortilla chips or tostada if you like.

Tip

When making ceviche, make sure you buy the freshest fish possible. Find out when the fish is delivered to your fishmonger, so you know the best day to buy it, and keep it in the fridge right up until you want to use it.

GREEN TEA VEGETABLE TEMPURA

I learned to make tempura when I was 16 from a Japanese chef at the first restaurant I worked in. The batter is very light, delicate and crisp – you can use it to deep-fry anything!

Preparation time: 20 minutes
Cooking time: 10 minutes

SERVES 4

INGREDIENTS

500g (1lb 2oz) mixed veggies (sweet potato, carrots, baby aubergines/eggplants, purple cauliflower and asparagus are great)
1 litre (32fl oz) vegetable or canola oil, for deep-frying
1 tsp sea salt mixed with 1 tsp Matcha green tea powder

For the dipping sauce
4 tbsp mirin
4 tbsp soy sauce
1 tbsp sweet chilli sauce
juice of 1 lemon

For the batter
1 egg yolk
3 ice cubes
180ml (6½fl oz) ice-cold water
50g (2oz/½ cup) cornflour or rice flour
65g (2¼oz/½ cup) plain (all-purpose) flour, plus extra for dusting
salt and pepper

1 Slice the vegetables or break them into small florets. The harder vegetables should be sliced about 5mm (¼in) thick, so they don't take too long to cook. Once they are all prepped, leave them at room temperature.

2 Mix together the ingredients for the dipping sauce and set aside.

3 Pour the oil into a large, deep saucepan, wok or a deep fryer. Heat to 170–185°C (340–360°F). If you don't have a kitchen thermometer, you can drizzle a little batter into the oil and if it immediately sizzles to the top it's hot enough.

4 While the oil is heating, make the batter. Place the egg yolk in a large bowl, add the ice to the water and use chopsticks to mix the iced water into the yolk. Slowly add the flours using four chopsticks – two in each hand – to gently stir it in. Do not over mix it – it's supposed to be only slightly mixed so the more lumps the merrier.

5 Place a couple of tablespoons of flour in a separate bowl and season with a pinch of salt and pepper. Coat a few of the vegetables in the flour then dip them into the batter, making sure they are well covered. Carefully lower them into the hot oil and fry for 2–2½ minutes. You can drizzle more of the batter over the vegetables using a spoon while they are frying to add more crunch. Be careful not to overcrowd the pan, as this brings down the temperature of the oil and you might end up with soggy, greasy tempura – you will probably need to cook the vegetables in 3 or 4 batches. Also make sure that the oil isn't too hot or the tempura might overcook. You will know it's cooked when the batter is golden and crisp all over; the vegetable should still have a little crunch.

6 Transfer the tempura to some kitchen paper to drain off any excess oil, sprinkle with the salt and Matcha powder mixture. Repeat with the rest of the veggies. Serve straightaway with the dipping sauce on the side.

MOZZARELLA FRITTERS WITH TGK FIG AND HONEY CHUTNEY

I'm afraid to say that I love deep-fried, crispy, hot bits of cheese . . . This dish is stepping away from the traditional brie and cranberry combo of old, and instead uses sexy mozzarella. It is served with our TGK fig and honey chutney. This is a really simple recipe, which is great because it means I can make it more often! The chutney can be made a few days ahead and kept in an airtight container in the fridge.

Preparation time: 20 minutes
Cooking time: 45 minutes to 1 hour

SERVES 4

INGREDIENTS

150g (5oz) fresh breadcrumbs
1 tsp garlic powder
2 tsp finely chopped flat-leaf parsley
600ml (1 pint) vegetable oil, for deep-frying
800g (1lb 10oz) mini mozzarella balls
100g (3½oz/¾ cup, plus 2 tbsp) plain
   (all-purpose) flour
2 eggs, lightly beaten
mixed salad leaves, to serve

For the chutney

400g (14oz) fresh figs, cut into
   1cm (½in) pieces
50g (2oz/¼ cup) caster sugar
100ml (3½fl oz) white wine vinegar
100g (3½oz) honey
1 banana shallot, peeled and finely diced

1 First make the chutney. Place the figs, sugar, vinegar, honey and shallots in a saucepan. Bring to the boil and then turn down the heat and leave to simmer for 45 minutes to 1 hour, until thick and glossy. Remove from the heat and leave to cool.

2 To make the breadcrumb mixture to coat the mozzarella balls, combine the breadcrumbs, garlic powder and parsley in a shallow bowl or on a plate.

3 Pour the oil into a deep saucepan or deep fryer and heat to 180°C (350°F). You can test whether the oil is hot enough by dropping in a small cube of bread. If it sizzles and turns golden within about 30 seconds, then you're ready to start cooking. While the oil is heating, place the mozzarella balls on a clean tea towel to drain.

4 Put the flour in a shallow bowl and the beaten eggs in a separate bowl. Dust the mozzarella balls first in the flour, then dip them in the egg wash and finally coat in the breadcrumbs. Carefully lower a few mozzarella balls into the hot oil and cook for 3–4 minutes until golden brown and crispy on the outside. Don't overcrowd the oil or it will cause the temperature to drop and you may end up with soggy breadcrumbs. Drain on kitchen paper while you cook the rest of the mozzarella.

5 Serve with the chutney and some mixed salad leaves.

"These mozzarella fritters are out of this world. We could eat them all day..."

CHILLI CRAB TOASTS

These days, crabmeat is easy to get hold of, even from the supermarket. Gone are the days of cracking shells and picking out the meat, making this a super simple light bite where all the hard work has been done for you.

Preparation time: 10 minutes
Cooking time: 5 minutes

INGREDIENTS

2 slices of sourdough bread
½ red chilli, de-seeded and finely chopped
zest and juice of 1 lime
3 tbsp mayonnaise
salt
150g (5oz) white crabmeat
2 tbsp roughly chopped coriander (cilantro)
30g (1oz) brown crabmeat
¼ Granny Smith apple

1 First get your sourdough toasting. Meanwhile, mix together the chilli, lime zest and half the juice in a bowl along with the mayonnaise. Season with a little salt.

2 Stir in the white crabmeat and half the chopped coriander.

3 Spread the toasted bread with the brown crabmeat and then top with the white meat mixture.

4 With the skin still on, finely slice the apple into matchsticks and pile some on top of the crab toasts. Finally, squeeze over a little more lime juice and scatter with the remaining coriander leaves.

"Gee's toasties are delicious – the perfect nibble for a dinner party."

HOT SMOKED SALMON TARTS WITH A PEA SHOOT, CORNICHON AND RADISH SALAD

Hot smoked salmon and crème fraîche cocooned in lovely buttery puff pastry and served with a simple, tasty salad that requires no pre-cooking, I hear you ask? Time to get on the phone and get some people round, don't you think? Tell them to pick up a bottle of something white and crisp on their way.

Preparation time: 30 minutes, plus 20 minutes to chill

Cooking time: 55 minutes

SERVES 4

INGREDIENTS
flour, for dusting
250g (9oz) all-butter puff pastry
2 large eggs, lightly beaten
120ml (4fl oz) crème fraîche
1 tsp horseradish sauce
a pinch of celery salt
freshly ground black pepper
1 tbsp chopped dill
1 tsp finely grated lemon zest
125g (4½oz) hot smoked salmon, flaked

For the salad
40g (1½oz) cocktail cornichons, sliced
2 shallots, peeled and thinly sliced into rings
125g (4½oz) radishes, cut into wedges
50g (2oz) pea shoots

For the dressing
1 tsp Dijon mustard
1½ tsp honey
2 tsp cider vinegar
4 tbsp olive oil
salt and pepper

1 Lightly dust your work surface with flour, then roll out the pastry to a thickness of about 5mm (¼in). Cut out 4 circles big enough to line 4 loose-bottomed 10cm x 3cm (4in x 1¼in) tart tins. Press the pastry into the base and side of the tins and prick the base several times with a fork. Trim off any excess overhanging pastry and chill in the fridge for about 20 minutes.

2 Preheat the oven to 180°C (350°F/gas 4) and place a baking sheet in the oven to heat up. When the pastry has rested, line each case with some greaseproof paper and fill with baking beans. Place on the hot baking sheet and cook for 30 minutes. Remove the beans and greaseproof paper and continue to cook for a further 5 minutes until the pastry is golden.

3 For the filling, beat together the eggs, crème fraîche and horseradish. Season with celery salt and freshly ground black pepper and mix in the dill and lemon zest. Divide the hot smoked salmon between the pastry cases then pour over the egg mixture. Place on the baking tray and cook in the oven for 18–20 minutes until just set and lightly golden.

4 To make the salad, toss together the cornichons, shallots, radishes and pea shoots.

5 To make the dressing, whisk together the mustard, honey and vinegar then slowly whisk in the oil. Season with salt and pepper. Add to the salad and toss gently to coat. Serve the warm tartlets with the salad.

BEEF CARPACCIO WITH LIGHTLY PICKLED CEPS AND TRUFFLE DRESSING

Beef carpaccio is a fantastic dinner party dish because you can get the mushrooms and beef ready ahead of time and then it's just a case of assembling it before your guests arrive. I love the flavours of wild mushrooms, truffle and Parmesan with beef, but experiment with whatever is in season. Don't worry about cutting the beef wafer thin: fillet is so tender that it's OK to be served slightly thicker.

Preparation time: 15 minutes, plus overnight to pickle and 30 minutes to 1 hour to chill

Cooking time: 15 minutes

SERVES 8

INGREDIENTS
500g (1lb 2oz) beef fillet
salt and pepper
1 head of radicchio, trimmed and leaves
    separated
1 head of yellow dandelion leaves
    (or chicory or more radicchio)
Parmesan cheese shavings, to serve

For the pickled mushrooms
300g (10½oz) cep mushrooms, halved
    (if ceps aren't in season, any mushroom
    can be used)
a splash of olive oil
200ml (7fl oz) good-quality red wine vinegar
2 banana shallots, peeled and finely diced

For the dressing
25ml (1fl oz) good-quality red wine vinegar
75ml (3fl oz) extra virgin olive oil
a pinch of caster sugar
1 tsp chopped black truffle from a jar
1 tsp truffle oil
flaked sea salt and freshly ground black pepper

1 The day before, make your pickled mushrooms. Fry the mushrooms with a little oil in a very hot pan for a few minutes, until golden brown then tip them into a bowl. Heat the vinegar in a small pan and pour it over the chopped shallots. Leave to cool for 10 minutes and then add to the mushrooms. Leave in the fridge overnight.

2 Heat a non-stick frying pan over a high heat until smoking hot. Season the beef well with salt and pepper. Put the beef in the pan and sear all over until well sealed and a crust has formed. This will take 8–10 minutes. Remove from the pan and leave to cool. When the beef has cooled (it doesn't need to be cold), roll it in cling film as tightly as possible to create a sausage shape. Seal at both ends like a cracker and chill in the fridge for 30 minutes to 1 hour.

3 Meanwhile, whisk together all the dressing ingredients in a small bowl until thoroughly combined and set aside.

4 When you are ready to serve, slice the beef as thinly as you can and arrange it carefully on a plate. Add some salad leaves and pickled mushrooms to the middle and drizzle over the truffle dressing. Finally, top with some Parmesan shavings.

CHICKEN LIVER PARFAIT WITH TGK CIDER JELLY AND TOASTED BRIOCHE

Nothing compares with homemade pâtés and parfaits. This simple but impressive dish is perfect for popping in the middle of the table with some good bread and wine or, in this case, cider to linger over with friends.

Preparation time: 40 minutes, plus overnight to chill

Cooking time: 1 hour 10 minutes

INGREDIENTS

100ml (3½fl oz) Madeira
100ml (3½fl oz) white port
100g (3½oz) shallots, peeled and
    finely chopped
4 fresh thyme sprigs, leaves picked and
    finely chopped
2 garlic cloves, peeled and crushed
50ml (2fl oz) cider brandy
600g (1lb 3oz) chicken livers, cleaned
    and trimmed
5 eggs
450g (1lb) unsalted butter, melted and
    kept warm
1 tsp sea salt
2 pinches of freshly ground black pepper

For the cider jelly
6 gelatin leaves
500ml (16fl oz) organic cider
200ml (3fl oz) apple juice

To serve
toasted brioche
micro herbs

1   Preheat the oven to 130°C (250°F/gas ½). Put the Madeira, port, shallots, thyme, garlic and cider brandy in a small saucepan and bring to the boil over a high heat. Let it bubble and reduce by one-third. Remove from the heat and set aside to cool.

2   Blitz the chicken livers with the cooled reduced alcohol mixture in a blender until smooth. Add the eggs, one at a time, blending for 3–4 minutes until the mixture is silky smooth. Gradually incorporate the warm melted butter. Season with the sea salt and black pepper.

3   Line the base of a large terrine mould with greaseproof paper. Pass the contents of the blender through a fine sieve into the mould, forcing the mixture through the sieve with the back of a ladle. Cover the surface with a piece of greaseproof paper and top with the lid of the terrine. If you don't have a terrine, you can use a 900g (2lb) loaf tin and cover it tightly with foil all over to make it waterproof.

4   Stand the terrine (or loaf tin) in a roasting tray and pour enough boiling water into the tray to come about two-thirds of the way up the side of the terrine. Cook in the oven for 45 minutes to 1 hour, until the terrine reaches 67–70°C (152–158°F) in the middle (test using a kitchen temperature probe). Remove from the oven, leave in the bain marie to cool, then chill overnight in the fridge.

5   To make the jelly, soak the gelatin leaves in cold water. Meanwhile, heat the cider in a saucepan for about 5 minutes, then remove from the heat. Squeeze the excess water from the gelatin and then stir it into the cider until dissolved. Mix in the apple juice. Line a shallow tray with cling film and then pour the liquid into the tray. Set in the fridge overnight.

6   Slice the parfait and arrange on a plate, decorate with cubes of the jelly and serve with toasted brioche and some micro herbs.

SMOKED SALMON AND RADISH FINGERS WITH DILL BUTTER

INGREDIENTS

75g (3oz) good-quality
   salted butter, softened
2 tbsp freshly chopped dill
finely grated zest of
   ½ lemon
a good squeeze of
   lemon juice
salt and pepper
10 thin or medium slices
   of brown or white bread
5–10 slices of smoked
   salmon (depending on
   their size)
6–8 radishes, very thinly
   sliced

1 Mix together the butter, dill, lemon zest and lemon juice. Season with a little salt and pepper, then spread on all of the slices of bread.

2 Place the smoked salmon and radishes on half of slices of the bread and top with the remaining slices. Trim away the crusts and cut each one into three fingers. Arrange on a pretty plate and serve. Don't forget to point your pinkies and chat about the neighbours and how variable the weather has been.

RARE ROAST BEEF WITH MUSTARD MAYONNAISE BAGUETTE

INGREDIENTS

1 small granary baguette
2 tbsp mayonnaise
1 tbsp wholegrain
   mustard
1 tsp English mustard
salt and pepper
4 slices of rare roast beef
   (leftovers from a roast
   are great, or slices from
   the deli)
3 tbsp TGK onion
   marmalade (see page 105)
a small bunch of
   watercress, thick
   stalks removed

1 Preheat the grill. Cut the baguettes in half lengthways and across the middle. Lightly toast the cut sides.

2 Mix together the mayonnaise and mustards and season with salt and pepper.

3 Spread the mayonnaise over each half of the baguette, then top with the roast beef and spoon over the onion marmalade. Finally, top with the watercress.

CRAB AND LEMON MAYONNAISE SANDWICH

INGREDIENTS

400g (14oz) white
    crabmeat
butter, for spreading
8 slices of wholemeal bread
optional: cress, to serve

For the homemade mayonnaise

1 egg yolk
1 tsp lemon juice
1 tsp white wine vinegar
½ tsp Dijon mustard
110ml (3½fl oz) canola,
    sunflower or a very
    light olive oil
1 heaped tsp lemon zest
a pinch of salt

1 Whisk together the egg yolk, lemon juice, vinegar and mustard for 30 seconds, until well blended. Add the oil a few drops at a time, whisking continuously. If you add it any quicker, the mayonnaise may split. SLOWLY. Once you've added about one-third of the oil and it has emulsified properly, you can add the oil in more of a stream. Whisk in the lemon zest and salt. Cover and chill in the fridge (it will keep up to a week).

2 Mix the crabmeat with 2–3 tablespoons of the lemony mayo.

3 Lightly butter the bread and spread half the slices with a thick layer of the crab. Top with the other pieces of bread, slice off the crusts and cut into triangles.

SAFFRON-SPICED CHICKEN, MANGO AND CORIANDER WRAP

INGREDIENTS

4 skinless, boneless chicken
    thighs
salt and pepper
4 white or wholemeal wraps
2 Little Gem lettuces
½ cucumber, thinly sliced
½ red onion, peeled and
    thinly sliced
½ mango, peeled and
    chopped

For the spice mix

a pinch of saffron; 2 tsp ground cumin; 2 tsp ground coriander; 1 tsp turmeric; 2 tsp garam masala; ½ tsp chilli powder; 1 tbsp Greek yoghurt

For the green yoghurt sauce

2 handfuls each of
    coriander (cilantro) and
    mint leaves
200ml (7fl oz) Greek yoghurt

1 Soak the saffron in 100ml (3fl oz) hot water then combine with the spice mix ingredients (including the saffron soaking water and the yoghurt). Pour over the chicken and leave to marinate for 2 hours.

2 To cook the chicken, preheat the oven to 190°C (375°F/gas 5). Blitz the herbs and yoghurt to make a bright green sauce.

3 Heat a griddle pan (or barbecue). Season the chicken and cook for 5 minutes on each side. Transfer to a baking tray and finish off in the oven for 5–10 minutes, until cooked through.

4 Place a couple of slices of lettuce on each wrap, followed by some cucumber and onion. Top with the chicken and mango, and drizzle with the green yoghurt. Roll up and serve.

VEGETARIAN

GRIDDLED AUBERGINES WITH CHICKPEAS, TOMATOES AND MOZZARELLA

Although I am not a vegetarian I do love eating vegetarian dishes, especially when travelling. They tend to be a little lighter than meaty main courses and cooked right, I don't miss the meat at all.

Preparation time: 15 minutes
Cooking time: 10 minutes

SERVES 4

INGREDIENTS

3–4 medium aubergines (eggplants), cut
   into discs 1–1.5cm (½–¾in) thick
3–4 tbsp olive oil, plus extra to drizzle
salt and pepper
1 garlic clove, peeled and sliced
a pinch of dried chilli flakes
400g (14oz) cherry tomatoes, halved
50ml (2fl oz) white wine
50ml (2fl oz) vegetable stock
400g (14oz) tin of chickpeas, rinsed
   and drained
2 balls of mozzarella
Parmesan cheese shavings, to serve
1 tbsp fresh thyme, flat-leaf parsley or basil,
   to garnish

For the breadcrumbs
4 slices of ciabatta
1 tbsp olive oil
1 tbsp thyme leaves, plus a few leaves
   to garnish

1 Preheat the grill and put a large frying pan on a high heat. Place the rounds of aubergine on a large baking tray. Drizzle with 2–3 tablespoons of oil and season with salt and pepper. Pop the tray under the grill and grill the aubergines for 2–4 minutes on each side, until golden brown.

2 Meanwhile, pour 1 tablespoon of oil into the hot frying pan and add the garlic. Fry for 30 seconds, then add the chilli flakes, halved tomatoes and the wine. Bring to a simmer then add the stock. Cook for 2 minutes until the tomatoes start to release their juices.

3 Check the aubergines and if they are cooked and golden brown, turn off the grill but leave them in the oven to keep warm.

4 Blend the ciabatta slices, oil and thyme in a blender until you have fine crumbs. Tip them into a clean frying pan and dry-fry over a medium heat for 2 minutes, until golden brown. Set to one side.

5 Add the chickpeas to the pan with the tomatoes and warm them through on a low heat. Divide between serving plates and top with the aubergine rounds. Tear over the mozzarella and scatter with the herby breadcrumbs, fresh herbs and a drizzle of oil.

BURRATA WITH CAPONATA AND CONFIT GARLIC TOASTS

Burrata is similar to mozzarella, but with a cream in the middle. It is very rich and very good. Caponata is a Sicilian dish made from vegetables cooked together in a luscious tomato sauce. It is finished with a splash of balsamic vinegar for an *agrodolce* – sweet and sour – flavour. Often served cool with cheese and cold meats, it is great with burrata and these garlicky toasts.

Preparation time: 15 minutes, plus cooling time

Cooking time: 40 minutes

SERVES 4

INGREDIENTS

2 bulbs of garlic
400ml (13fl oz) light olive oil, plus extra
    to drizzle
4 slices of sourdough bread
4 x 150g (5oz) burrata or mozzarella balls
salt and pepper

For the caponata

100ml (3½fl oz) olive oil
1 aubergine (eggplant), diced into 1cm
    (½in) pieces
4 sticks of celery, diced into 1cm (½in) pieces
1 red (bell) pepper, diced into 1cm (½in) pieces
1 red onion, peeled and diced into 1cm
    (½in) pieces
200g (7oz) tin of chopped tomatoes
100g (3½oz) sultanas
salt and pepper
50ml (2fl oz) balsamic vinegar
50g (2oz) toasted pine nuts
a small bunch of basil

1 First make the confit garlic paste for the toasts. Place the whole garlic bulbs in a small saucepan and cover in the oil. Cook over a very low heat for 40 minutes, then leave to cool. When completely cooled, remove the garlic bulbs from the oil, squeeze out the flesh from the cloves and mash to a paste. If you want the purée to be totally smooth, you can pass it through a sieve.

2 Meanwhile, heat half the oil for the caponata in a large saucepan over a high heat and quickly fry the aubergine for about 5 minutes. Reduce the heat, pour in the remaining oil and add the celery, pepper and onion. Cook for a few minutes until just starting to soften, then add the tomatoes and sultanas and simmer for 20 minutes, until thickened. Season, to taste, with salt and pepper, then stir through the balsamic vinegar and the pine nuts. Finally, add the basil and leave to cool.

3 Toast the bread and spread a little of the garlic purée on top. Serve the toasts alongside the burrata with a large spoonful of caponata. Drizzle the burrata with a little oil and season it well with salt and pepper.

Tip

The oil used for cooking the garlic will have a wonderfully infused flavour. I often make large batches of it and store the oil to use in cooking.

TWICE-BAKED GOAT'S CHEESE SOUFFLÉS

This is based on my mother's 'go-to' recipe for dinner parties. Some would say that baking a soufflé twice amounts to cheating, but I believe it has a far nicer texture as a result: more flavour and slightly less air. This is a truly delicious, light starter, and most of the work can be done a couple of days ahead, which also makes for a relaxed host. If you want to make four, just halve the ingredients.

Preparation time: 35 minutes, plus 25 minutes cooling

Cooking time: 40 minutes

SERVES 8

INGREDIENTS

100g (3½oz) butter, plus 2 tbsp, melted
2 tbsp finely chopped roasted hazelnuts (best done in a blender)
50g (2oz) finely grated Parmesan cheese
100g (3½oz/¾ cup, plus 2 tbsp) plain (all-purpose) flour
600ml (1 pint) goat's milk
1 tsp Dijon mustard
4 egg yolks, plus 5 egg whites
1 tsp fresh thyme leaves
200g (7oz) rindless goat's cheese, crumbled
8 tbsp TGK onion marmalade (see page 105), to serve

For the glaze
2 egg yolks
100ml (3½fl oz) double (heavy) cream
3 tbsp finely grated Parmesan cheese
25g (1oz) goat's cheese, crumbled

For the rocket salad
1 tbsp Dijon mustard
2 tbsp white wine vinegar
5 tbsp olive oil
salt and pepper
150g (5oz) rocket (arugula) leaves
1 Conference pear

1 Preheat the oven to 180°C (350°F/gas 4). Brush the insides of 8 x 200ml (7fl oz) ramekins with the 2 tablespoons of melted butter.

2 Mix together the hazelnuts and 2 tablespoons of the Parmesan. Tip into one of the ramekins. Roll it around until the sides are covered then tap and tip into the next ramekin. Repeat until all 8 ramekins are coated on the inside.

3 Melt the 100g (3½oz) butter in a medium-sized saucepan. Add the flour and mix well. Stir continuously for 2 minutes to cook the flour, then remove from the heat and gradually whisk in half the milk – using a whisk will help to prevent lumps. Return the saucepan to the heat and add the rest of the milk. Bring to the boil, mixing all the time to prevent lumps. As soon as it starts to boil, transfer the sauce to a bowl and leave to cool slightly.

4 Beat in the mustard, egg yolks, thyme and the rest of the Parmesan, then fold in the crumbled goat's cheese.

5 In a separate bowl, whisk the egg whites until stiff peaks form. Gradually fold these into the goat's cheese mixture.

6 Divide between the prepared ramekins and place them in a deep roasting tray. Fill the tray halfway up the sides of the ramekins with boiling or very hot water and bake in the oven for 15–20 minutes until risen and golden brown. Once cooked, carefully remove the ramekins from the roasting tray and leave to cool. (At this stage they can be kept in the fridge for up to a couple of days, or they can be frozen for up to a month. Defrost before cooking.)

7 When ready to serve, carefully run a thin blade knife around the edges of the soufflés and tip them out into an ovenproof dish. The bottoms will now become the tops. Preheat the oven to 180°C (350°F/gas 4).

8 Mix together the glaze ingredients, keeping the goat's cheese to one side. Spoon the glaze on top of the soufflés and scatter over the cheese. Cook in the oven for 10 minutes. Remove from the oven and leave to cool.

9 While they are cooling, make the rocket salad. Mix together the mustard and vinegar then gradually whisk in the oil. Whisk in 1 teaspoon of warm water to help it emulsify. Season well with salt and pepper.

10 Pick off and discard the thick stalks from the rocket. Keeping the skin on, cut thin slices from the pear, then cut these into matchsticks. Toss the rocket leaves and pear together in the dressing.

11 Serve the salad alongside the cooled soufflés with a spoonful of onion marmalade.

TRIPLE MUSHROOM, STILTON, LEEK AND WALNUT EN CROUTE

This is ideal to serve at a get-together when you have a mixture of meat-eaters and vegetarians – it saves you cooking two different dishes and I promise you that everyone will leave satisfied.

Preparation time: 45 minutes, plus 30 minutes chilling

Cooking time: 45 minutes

SERVES 4

INGREDIENTS

20g (¾oz) dried porcini mushrooms
50g (2oz/⅓ cup) walnut pieces
2 tbsp olive oil, plus extra for drizzling
25g (1oz) butter
110g (4oz) portobello mushrooms, cut into 1–2cm (½–¾in) pieces
110g (4oz) baby or small chestnut mushrooms, quartered
1 leek, thinly sliced
4 garlic cloves, peeled and crushed
1 tbsp fresh thyme leaves
finely grated zest of 1 lemon
150g (5oz) Stilton cheese, crumbled into small pieces
4 tbsp crème fraîche
salt and pepper
flour, for dusting
500g (1lb 2oz) all-butter puff pastry
1 large egg, beaten with 1 tbsp milk
1 tsp poppy seeds, for sprinkling
4 vines of cherry tomatoes (each with roughly 6 tomatoes attached)
steamed green vegetables, to serve

1   Pour hot water over the dried porcini mushrooms and leave for 30 minutes so that they plump up. Remove from the liquid and roughly chop the mushrooms.

2   Meanwhile, heat a large frying pan over a medium heat and lightly toast the walnut pieces for 2–3 minutes until they take on a darker golden colour. Tip on to a plate and set aside.

3   Return the pan to the heat and add 1 tablespoon of the oil and half of the butter. Once the butter is bubbling, add the portobello and chestnut mushrooms. Cook over a medium to high heat for about 8 minutes, until they are softened and lightly golden. Transfer to a large bowl.

4   Return the pan to the heat and add the remaining oil and butter. Once the butter is bubbling, sauté the leeks and garlic for about 5 minutes until the leeks are softened. Stir in the thyme leaves, lemon zest and chopped porcini mushrooms. Toss around in the pan, then transfer to the bowl with the cooked mushrooms. Leave to cool. Once cool, mix in the walnuts, Stilton and crème fraîche and season with salt and pepper.

5   Lightly flour your work surface and then thinly roll out the pastry and cut into 8 equal-sized pieces – squares, rectangles or circles, it's up to you. Lightly brush the edges of 4 pieces of pastry with the beaten egg and then divide the mushroom filling between them, leaving a 5mm–1cm (¼–½in) border of pastry. Lay a second piece of pastry on the top of each one, and seal with the handle of a teaspoon. Trim the edges of the pastry with a sharp knife to give a neat finish.

6   Score diagonal lines over the top of the pastry and pierce a small hole in the top of each one to let out the steam as it cooks. Transfer to a lightly greased baking tray, brush with egg wash and scatter over the poppy seeds. Chill for 30 minutes. Preheat the oven to 200°C (400°F/gas 6).

7   Bake for 30 minutes until golden. While the parcels are cooking, place the tomato vines on a separate baking tray. Drizzle with a little oil and season with salt and pepper. Pop in the oven and cook with the parcels for 10 minutes, until the tomatoes start to burst open. Serve the pastry parcels with the roasted tomatoes and a medley of green vegetables.

BEETROOT TARTE TATIN WITH CANDIED BEET AND GOAT'S CHEESE SALAD

Beetroot and goat's cheese is a bit of a match made in heaven. Here, with the buttery pastry, sweet shallots and crisp salad they work together wonderfully. The tarts can be made ahead and cooked straight from the fridge.

Preparation time: 25 minutes
Cooking time: 45 minutes

SERVES 4

INGREDIENTS

For the tarts

4 banana shallots, peeled and sliced
25g (1oz) butter, plus extra for greasing
1 tsp brown sugar
3 sprigs of thyme
500g (1lb 2 oz) pre-rolled puff pastry
4 large cooked beetroots, thinly sliced
olive oil and aged balsamic vinegar, to drizzle

For the salad

4 small yellow beets
4–6 small candy stripe beets or regular
    baby beets
olive oil
salt and pepper
200g (7oz) fresh goat's cheese
a small handful of micro watercress

For the caramelized pecans

100g (3fl oz) pecan nuts
2 tbsp demerara (raw) sugar

1 Put the shallots, butter, sugar and thyme in a saucepan over a low heat and cook very gently for 30 minutes so that the onions caramelize. Remove from the heat and leave to cool.

2 Meanwhile, put the yellow beetroots for the salad in a saucepan and cover with water. Bring to the boil, simmer for 30 minutes, until cooked through, then drain and leave to cool. Rub off the skin with kitchen paper. Peel and very thinly slice the candy stripe beetroot using a mandolin. Dress with some oil and season with salt and pepper.

3 Grease 4 small ovenproof frying pans or 4 x 12cm (4½in) round tins with butter. Cut out 4 circles from the pastry just smaller than the base of the pans or tins. Arrange the sliced large beetroots in the base of each one in a flower shape and top with a spoonful of the shallots. Top with the pastry circle and press down the edges. Pierce with a fork.

4 Preheat the oven to 180°C (350°F/gas 4). Cook the tarts in the oven for 15 minutes, until the pastry is puffed up and golden brown. While the tarts are cooking put the pecans in a saucepan with the demerara sugar and cook gently for about 5 minutes, until the sugar has melted and coated the nuts. Run a knife around the edge of the tarts and turn them out on to serving plates. Arrange the yellow and candied beets on top with the goat's cheese, pecans and watercress. Drizzle with oil and balsamic vinegar, and serve.

THAI GREEN CURRY

This is one of those dishes that tastes even better the next day, once the flavours have had time to develop, so if you're having friends over, prepare it a day ahead and keep it in the fridge. It's quite fiery! If you don't want it so hot, use fewer chillies in the paste, chop up the rest and scatter them over the curry at the end for those that want some extra heat.

Preparation time: 20 minutes
Cooking time: 25 minutes

SERVES 4–6

INGREDIENTS
440ml (13fl oz) tin of coconut milk
1 tbsp fish sauce
1 tbsp palm sugar (or light brown sugar)
500g (1lb 2oz) mixed veggies (cubes of
    butternut squash, baby aubergines/
    eggplants, halved lengthways, baby corn
    and green beans go well together)
a small handful of Thai sweet basil
    (or regular will do)
steamed jasmine rice, to serve

For the curry paste
2 tsp coriander (cilantro) seeds
1 tsp cumin seeds
1 tsp white peppercorns
½ tsp turmeric
5 long green chillies, de-seeded and
    roughly chopped
3 small green bird's eye chillies, de-seeded
    and roughly chopped
2 stalks of lemon grass, roughly chopped
4 shallots, peeled and roughly chopped
3 garlic cloves, peeled and roughly chopped
3cm (1¼in) piece of galangal, roughly
    chopped (or you can use freshly grated ginger)
3 Kaffir lime leaves
a large handful of coriander (cilantro)
a pinch of salt

1 First make your curry paste. Dry-fry the coriander seeds, cumin seeds and white peppercorns in a small pan for 2–3 minutes, until their flavours are released. Grind them with the turmeric in a pestle and mortar or a spice grinder. Tip the ground spices into a food processor and add the rest of the paste ingredients. Add 4 tablespoons of water and whiz until smooth. (The paste can be kept in the fridge in an airtight container for up to 1 month – top it with some oil to stop the air getting in.)

2 Spoon the top third of the tin of coconut milk – the very creamy part – into a wok or saucepan set over a low to medium heat. Cook for 3–4 minutes, until it starts to thicken and the oil begins to separate out. (Coconut milk has a high fat content, so you don't need any extra oil.) Stir in your curry paste and cook for 3 minutes.

3 Keeping the heat fairly low, add the rest of the coconut milk, 125ml (4fl oz) water, the fish sauce and sugar. Add any harder vegetables first, like the squash, and leave to simmer gently for 6–8 minutes. Follow with the aubergines and baby corn, and cook for 3 minutes. Then add the green beans and simmer until the vegetables have cooked through. Just before serving with the steamed rice, stir through the basil leaves.

"Thai green curry is one of Gee's favourite things to eat, and Caroline's is no exception!"

FISH & SEAFOOD

FISH AND CHIPS

A good old English classic! Nothing beats a great fish and chip supper when my British side is calling for some comfort food. I never used to be a fan of mushy peas until I tried them with mint, and then I was hooked!

Preparation time: 10 minutes
Cooking time: 20–30 minutes, depending on the size of your fryer

INGREDIENTS

1½l (48fl oz) vegetable, sunflower or
   canola oil
4 x 180–200g (6–7oz) fillets of white fish
   (e.g. sustainable cod, plaice or haddock)
flour for dusting
salt and pepper
1 x quantity of delicious TGK chips (see
   page 100)
vinegar, to serve

For the minted peas

300g (10½oz) peas
optional: 750ml (24fl oz) vegetable stock
1 heaped tbsp freshly chopped mint leaves
1 tbsp butter
a pinch salt
¼ tsp caster sugar
1 tsp lemon juice
2 tbsp double (heavy) cream

For the batter

150g (5oz/1¼ cup) self-raising flour
55g (2oz) cornflour
1½ tsp baking powder
salt and pepper
354ml (12fl oz) bottle of beer

1   First cook the peas for 3 minutes in a pan of boiling water or vegetable stock. Drain well then return the peas to the pan, add the rest of the minted peas' ingredients and mash together with a potato masher or a fork.

2   Heat the oil in a large pan to 190°C (375°F). If you don't have a kitchen thermometer, you can test the oil is hot enough by dropping in a small cube of bread. It should fizz and turn brown within about 30 seconds. Preheat the oven to 140°C (275°F/gas 1).

3   While the oil is heating, make the batter. Use a whisk to mix together the flours, baking powder, salt and pepper in a large bowl. Pour in half of the beer and whisk it in lightly and roughly. You need the mixture to just come together – don't worry if there are a few lumps. Keep adding more beer until it is has the consistency of very thick double cream. To test the consistency, dip your finger in it. Your finger should stay well coated with batter when you pull it out of the mixture. I added all but a swig of beer from my bottle.

4   Put 3–4 tablespoons of flour on a plate. Pat dry the fish fillets with kitchen paper and lightly season them with salt and pepper. Then roll the fish in the flour to coat them all over.

5   Next, dunk one fish fillet in the batter, making sure it is completely covered, and then lower it carefully into the hot oil. Cook for 5–6 minutes, using tongs to turn the fish over halfway through. The batter should be golden and crisp on the outside and the fish should be opaque all the way through. Depending on the size of your pan you will probably be able to cook only 1 or 2 fillets at a time – don't overcrowd the pan or the oil temperature will reduce and make your batter soggy and greasy.

6   Lift out the fish and drain it on kitchen paper. Keep the cooked fish on a tray in the oven while you cook the rest. Serve with plenty of hot chips, a dash of vinegar and the mushy minted peas.

PAN-FRIED SEA BASS WITH SAUTÉED LEEKS, CRISPY BACON AND GARLIC CREAM SAUCE

Sea bass was one of the first things I learned to cook properly at cookery school – mainly because it is quite expensive and so there was no room for error! Its flesh is delicate and sweet and the skin goes perfectly crisp. If you cook it skin-side down for 80 per cent of the cooking time, then just simply flip it over and let the residual heat finish it off, it won't over cook and dry out.

Preparation time: 20 minutes
Cooking time: 1 1/4 hours

SERVES 4

INGREDIENTS

1 bulb of garlic
4 tbsp olive oil, plus 1 tsp
2 sprigs of fresh thyme
salt and pepper
200ml (7fl oz) double (heavy) cream
100ml (3 1/2fl oz) chicken stock
12 baby leeks, trimmed
200g (7oz) smoked bacon lardons
1 tbsp finely chopped flat-leaf parsley
4 x 125g (4 1/2oz) sea bass fillets, pin-
    boned and de-scaled but skin left on
25g (1oz) butter
a dash of lemon juice

1 Preheat the oven to 190°C (375°F/gas 5). Peel away the thick outer skins from the garlic bulb, leaving the last few softer layers around the cloves. Cut off a little from the top of the bulb just to expose the inner cloves.

2 Place the bulb on a piece of foil along with 2 tablespoons of oil, the thyme and a little salt and pepper, then wrap it up. Place on a baking tray and roast in the oven for about 45 minutes, or until it feels soft when lightly pressed. Unwrap and leave to cool, then pop out the cloves.

3 Heat the cream in a saucepan with the stock and roasted garlic. Simmer gently for 15 minutes, then tip into a food processor and blend until smooth. Strain through a sieve.

4 Bring a large pan of salted water to the boil and blanch the leeks for 1 minute. Plunge into ice-cold water, then drain well.

5 Place 2 large frying pans on a high heat and a small pan on a medium heat. Fry the bacon in 1 teaspoon of oil in the small pan until crisp, then drain off the excess oil and stir in the parsley. Set aside.

6 Meanwhile, add 1 tablespoon of oil to each large frying pan. Season the skin of the sea bass fillets with a little salt then place them skin-side down in the pans. Cook for 4 minutes, or until the skin is crisp and the fish is almost cooked through, then turn the fillets over, remove from the heat and set aside.

7 In a separate pan, fry the leeks in the butter for 2 minutes until they start to take on some colour. Season with lemon juice, salt and pepper.

8 Serve the leeks topped with the sea bass, skin-side up. Scatter with the crispy bacon lardons and spoon the garlic cream around the fish.

MUSSELS IN BRITISH CIDER CREAM WITH GARLIC LADDER BREADS

Mussels are very easy to cook and they always remind me of childhood holidays by the sea. Moules marinière holds a special place in my heart, but this recipe is a simple British twist on the classic French dish.

Preparation time: 25 minutes, plus 1–2 hours resting

Cooking time: 15 minutes

SERVES 4

INGREDIENTS

50g (2oz) unsalted butter
2 banana shallots, peeled and finely diced
2 sticks of celery, finely diced
2 garlic cloves, peeled and finely sliced
1 tbsp fresh thyme leaves
2kg (4lb 6oz) mussels, cleaned and de-
    bearded (discard any that are open)
300ml (10fl oz) dry British cider
150ml (5fl oz) double (heavy) cream
2 tbsp finely chopped flat-leaf parsley
salt and pepper

For the bread

500g (1lb 2oz/4 cups) strong white flour,
    plus extra for dusting
10g ($^{1}/_{3}$oz) fresh yeast or 5g ($^{1}/_{6}$oz)
    dried yeast
1 tsp salt
1 tsp caster sugar
about 350ml (11fl oz) warm water
50g (2oz) butter
1 large garlic clove, peeled and crushed

1   First make your bread. Place the flour in a large bowl and either rub in the fresh yeast or stir in the dried yeast. Add the salt and sugar. Pour in most of the warm water and start mixing together using the handle of a wooden spoon and then your hands, adding more water if you need it, to form a smooth ball of dough.

2   Turn out the dough on to a lightly floured surface and knead for 10 minutes, or until the dough is smooth and comes away from the surface without sticking. Return the dough to the mixing bowl and cover with a tea towel. Leave in a warm place for 1–2 hours, until doubled in size.

3   Preheat the oven to 220°C (400°F/gas 6) and place a baking tray in the oven to heat up. Turn out the dough on to a well-floured surface, taking care not to deflate it. It will spread out over the surface. Generously flour the top of the dough, then cover with a clean tea towel and rest for 5 minutes.

4   Using a knife or plastic scraper, divide the dough into 2 long rectangles. Divide each of these into 3 triangles by cutting them on the diagonal. Make 3 smaller cuts across the middle of each piece, about 2.5cm (1in) from the edge, cutting through to the work surface. Gently open out the holes with your fingers, so it looks like a ladder, and shake off the excess flour. Lift the dough pieces on to the hot baking tray and bake in the oven for 10–12 minutes, until golden brown.

5   While the breads are in the oven, melt the butter for the mussels in a large pan with a tight-fitting lid over a medium heat. Add the shallots, celery, garlic and thyme and cook for 5 minutes until soft and sweet. Turn up the heat and add the mussels and cider. Quickly cover with a lid and leave for 3 minutes, giving the pan a good shake every now and then.

6   Meanwhile, melt the butter for the bread in a pan and add the garlic. Once the breads are cooked, brush them with the butter. (If you have made the breads in advance and they have cooled, warm them through in the oven for 5 minutes, then brush with the butter.)

7   After the mussels have been cooking for 3 minutes, remove the lid and stir in the cream. Allow everything to come back up to a simmer and then stir in the parsley. Season with salt and pepper, and serve immediately.

MISO-GLAZED SALMON WITH LIGHTLY PICKLED CUCUMBER AND RED ONION SLAW

Miso is a fantastic ingredient to get into using. It's basically fermented bean paste and it is available in many forms. I use sweet white miso paste for this marinade, which is great with all sorts of ingredients – pork belly and lamb chops particularly benefit from this glaze, so experiment at home. The lightly pickled salad cuts through the richness of the oily fish perfectly.

Preparation time: 10 minutes, plus at least 1 hour marinating

Cooking time: 10 minutes

INGREDIENTS

4 x 150g (5oz) salmon fillets
1 tbsp black sesame seeds, to garnish
optional: nasturtium flowers, to garnish
optional: steamed rice, to serve

For the marinade

2 tbsp soy sauce
2 tsp mirin
1 tsp honey
3 tbsp sweet white miso paste

For the pickled cucumber and red onion

50g (2oz/¼ cup) caster sugar
200ml (7fl oz) rice wine vinegar
½ red onion, peeled and finely sliced
½ cucumber, de-seeded and finely sliced
50g (2oz) pickled pink ginger

1 First make the marinade by heating the soy sauce, mirin and honey in a small saucepan. Whisk in the miso paste, then remove from the heat and leave to cool. Place the salmon fillets in a dish and spread the marinade over the top. Leave to marinate in the fridge for at least an hour or overnight.

2 Heat the sugar and vinegar in a saucepan and simmer until the sugar has dissolved. Remove from the heat and add the red onion. Let it cool and then pour over the cucumber. Finally stir in the pink ginger and chill until needed.

3 Preheat the grill to high. Transfer the salmon fillets to a baking tray, spoon over any marinade and grill for 8–10 minutes, until caramelized around the edges and cooked through. Serve with some of the pickled salad and decorate with black sesame seeds and nasturtium flowers, if using.

"Sophie's dish is simple, elegant and healthy – the perfect TGK dinner!"

"Putting together the restaurant and this cookery book has had its challenges, but we all have the same goal: to do our best to ensure our customers are happy and well fed!"

BAKED COD AND BROWN SHRIMPS WITH LEMON AND CHILLI

I have used cod in this recipe but only do so if you can get fish that is sourced sustainably. If you can't, try a less popular white fish such as pollock or ling. The salting technique used here firms up the texture of the fish, helping it to stay together when cooked.

Preparation time: 5 minutes, plus 30 minutes resting

Cooking time: 15 minutes

SERVES 4

INGREDIENTS

8 tbsp rock salt
zest of 2 lemons, plus 1 lemon cut into
    8 slices
4 x 200g (7oz) cod fillets, skin removed
    and pin-boned
olive oil, for greasing
a dash of white wine

For the shrimps

50g (2oz) unsalted butter
½ red chilli, de-seeded and finely chopped
150g (5oz) brown shrimps
salt and pepper
juice of ½–1 lemon, to taste
1 tbsp finely chopped parsley

To serve

boiled or steamed new potatoes or
    mashed potatoes and green veg

1   Mix the salt and lemon zest together. Line a deep baking tray or roasting tin with a long piece of cling film (this just helps contain the salt) making sure there is lots hanging over the edge. Scatter half the salt mixture over the base and then place the fish fillets on top. Scatter over the rest of the lemony salt and wrap the fish tightly in the cling film. Leave for 30 minutes to draw out some of the water. Preheat the oven to 190°C (375°F/gas 5).

2   Remove the fish from the salt and rinse well under cold water. Pat dry with kitchen paper.

3   Grease the bottom of an ovenproof dish with a little oil, then place the fish on top. Cover in the lemon slices and pour the white wine into the dish. Roast in the oven for 12–15 minutes or until the fish is cooked through.

4   While the fish is in the oven, melt the butter over a medium heat and add the chilli. Cook for a couple of minutes before stirring in the shrimps and warming through.

5   When the cod is cooked, remove from the oven and add any cooking juices to the butter and shrimps. Taste the shrimps, season if necessary, and add a good squeeze of lemon juice and the chopped parsley. Serve with some simply cooked potatoes and green veg.

FRESH TUNA NIÇOISE WITH SLOW-ROASTED HERITAGE TOMATOES AND QUAILS' EGGS

There are so many variations on the French salad Niçoise: some with tuna, some without, some with potatoes, some without, and don't even get me started on anchovies, eggs and French beans! It seems there really is no recipe that is the same, so do bear that in mind with my version, and if you want to swap and change some of the ingredients to suit your taste then crack on.

Preparation time: 20 minutes
Cooking time: 2 hours

SERVES 4

INGREDIENTS

12–15 heritage tomatoes, each about the
    size of a golf ball
olive oil, for drizzling
salt and pepper
4 x 150–175g (5–6oz) fresh tuna steaks
12–16 Charlotte potatoes
12 quails' eggs, at room temperature
150g (5oz) French beans, tops trimmed
2 small lettuces, such as Little Gem, torn
    into pieces
1/3 cucumber, halved, de-seeded and sliced
1 banana shallot, peeled and finely sliced
a large handful of good-quality de-stoned
    black olives
1 tbsp small capers, drained

For the dressing

1 small garlic clove, peeled and cut in half
a pinch of coarse sea salt
3 anchovies in oil, roughly chopped
8 basil leaves, torn into pieces
6 tbsp extra virgin olive oil
1 tbsp red wine vinegar
1 tsp Dijon mustard
freshly ground black pepper

1 Preheat the oven to 110°C (225°F/gas 1/4). Place the tomatoes cut-side up on a baking tray lined with baking parchment. Drizzle with a little oil to give them a slight glisten, then scatter over some salt and pepper. Cook in the oven for about 2 hours. When they are ready, the tomatoes will be shrivelled and quite dry but still a little juicy in the middle – they may need a little more or less time depending on their size. Remove from the oven and cool to room temperature.

2 To make the dressing, pound the garlic to a paste with the coarse sea salt in a pestle and mortar. Pound in the anchovies and basil and finally mix in the oil, vinegar, mustard and a twist of black pepper. Transfer to a clean jar with a lid and set aside.

3 Remove the tuna from the fridge and allow it to come up to room temperature while you prepare the salad.

4 Cook the potatoes in boiling salted water for 8–10 minutes, until just tender. Drain and leave to cool slightly, then cut in half and set aside.

5 Meanwhile, cook the quails' eggs in boiling water for 1 1/2 minutes, then remove with a slotted spoon and plunge into a bowl of ice-cold water to stop them cooking. Drain, peel and set aside.

6 Boil the French beans in salted water for a few minutes until just tender, then plunge into ice-cold water, drain and set aside.

7 Brush the tuna with a little oil, and season with salt and pepper. Heat a griddle or frying pan until it is almost smoking. Cook the tuna steaks for 1 1/2–2 minutes on each side. Cook for a little longer if you like your tuna more well done.

8 In a separate frying pan, heat a glug of oil and fry the potatoes until they are lightly golden. Sprinkle with salt and drain on kitchen paper.

9 Put the lettuce leaves, cucumber, shallot, olives, capers, oven-roasted tomatoes and French beans in a large bowl. Shake the dressing and add half to the salad. Toss to coat then divide between 4 serving plates or bowls.

10 Halve the quails' eggs and add to the salad with the potatoes. Top with the tuna, either sliced or left whole. Spoon over some more dressing and serve.

PRAWN AND SCALLOPS WITH A DELICATE PONZU DRESSING ON A BED OF SHAVED VEGETABLES

I am a big fan of shellfish and I like to keep it simple so I can enjoy their subtle flavours. The ponzu dressing is fresh and flavourful but it won't overpower the scallops and prawns.

Preparation time: 15 minutes
Cooking time: 10 minutes

SERVES 4

INGREDIENTS
1 tbsp peanut oil
1 tbsp butter
12 raw king prawns, shelled and de-veined
8 jumbo scallops, roe removed
a pinch of salt

For the ponzu dressing
4 tbsp light soy sauce
juice of 1 lime
juice of 1 pink grapefruit
3 tbsp brown sugar
2 tbsp finely grated fresh ginger
2 tsp Worcestershire sauce

For the vegetables
2 carrots, peeled
½ cucumber
4 radishes
a handful of micro greens

1 Mix together all ingredients for the dressing in a small saucepan. Bring to the boil over a medium heat and cook for 2 minutes, until the sauce has reduced and thickened. Set aside.

2 Use a mandolin or a vegetable peeler to shave the carrots, cucumber and radishes into very fine strips. Place them all in a large bowl with the micro greens. Toss with a generous tablespoon of the dressing.

3 To cook the prawns and scallops, heat the oil in a frying pan over a medium heat and add the butter. Place the scallops and prawns in the pan and season with salt. Cook for 1–2 minutes on each side, depending on how thick they are. Remove the prawns as soon as they are opaque and a lovely pink colour. Then remove the scallops.

4 Place a handful of the vegetables in the middle of your serving plates, arrange the scallops and prawns on top, and finish with a drizzle of the dressing.

Tip

If you want a more filling meal, this goes very well on top of a bed of soba noodles.

CHICKEN
& GAME BIRDS

PAN-FRIED CHICKEN BREASTS WITH CHORIZO CRUMB AND PARMESAN POLENTA

Chicken breasts are one of the easiest things to over-cook, and there's nothing worse than dry, tough meat. But rather than hacking into each one and checking the middle, all you need to do is give it a press on its thickest part. If it feels firm and not springy, then it's cooked. Easy!

Preparation time: 20 minutes
Cooking time: 30 minutes

SERVES 4

INGREDIENTS

4 skin-on chicken breasts, trimmed
salt and pepper
2 tbsp olive oil
2 garlic cloves, unpeeled, lightly crushed
    with the flat of a knife
a few sprigs of thyme
25g unsalted butter
150g (5oz) chorizo sausage, sliced into 10
    pieces each 5mm (¼in) thick

For the chorizo crumb
125g (4½oz) chorizo sausage, skin removed,
    sliced into thick pieces
25g (1oz) skinless almonds
20g (¾oz) fresh breadcrumbs
1 tsp fresh thyme leaves

For the polenta
500ml (16fl oz) chicken stock
250ml (8fl oz) whole (full-cream) milk
175g (6oz) quick-cook polenta
40g (1½oz) butter
40g (1½oz) finely grated Parmesan cheese
salt and white pepper

For the sauce
400ml (13fl oz) dark chicken stock, reduced
    to 100ml (3½fl oz) over a low heat
1 tbsp freshly chopped parsley

1 Remove the chicken from the fridge 30 minutes before cooking. Preheat the oven to 190°C (375°F/gas 5).

2 First make the chorizo crumb by frying the chorizo pieces in a dry pan over a medium heat for 4 minutes, until the lovely oil has been released and the chorizo is crisp. Place the chorizo (retaining the oil in the pan) in a food processor along with the almonds and blend to form crumbs. Add the breadcrumbs and thyme leaves and pulse once more. Tip the mixture into a clean frying pan and lightly toast over a low to medium heat until crispy. Remove from the heat and set aside.

3 Heat a large, ovenproof frying pan over a high heat. Season the chicken with salt and pepper. Pour the oil into the pan then add the chicken, skin-side down. Cook for 5 minutes, until the skin is golden brown and crispy then turn over and add the garlic, thyme and butter. Cook for 1 minute.

4 Add the chorizo slices to the pan, then transfer the pan to the oven and cook for 6–8 minutes, until the chicken feels firm when pressed at its thickest part. Remove from the oven and leave to rest for 5 minutes.

5 While the chicken is resting, bring the stock and milk to the boil in a saucepan. Add the polenta and cook for 5 minutes whisking continuously. Once it starts to thicken and bubble, remove from the heat and whisk in the butter and Parmesan. Season with salt and white pepper.

6 Warm the reserved chorizo oil and stir in the reduced chicken stock and chopped parsley.

7 Cut the chicken breasts in half on an angle and serve on top of mounds of the polenta. Top with a few slices of chorizo then sprinkle over the chorizo crumb and finish with a drizzle of the sauce.

Tip

If you can buy chicken breasts with the wing attached, then these are perfect for this recipe.

MALAYSIAN CHICKEN SATAY WITH STICKY RICE AND CUCUMBER SALAD

Being half-Malaysian I had to share one of my family's all-time favourite recipes: my grandmother's chicken satay. I make this a lot at barbecues, and the aroma of satay cooking over hot coals always reminds me of visiting my family. When we arrive in Malaysia, our first stop is always to go and eat – you can find small vendors cooking satay by the roadside or in food courts all over the country.

Preparation time: 25 minutes, plus 2–8 hours marinating/soaking

Cooking time: 30 minutes

SERVES 4

INGREDIENTS

For the marinade
2 shallots or ½ small onion, peeled and roughly chopped
1 tsp chilli powder
3 tsp ground coriander (cilantro)
2 tsp ground cumin
1 tsp turmeric
2 tsp fennel seeds
3 garlic cloves, peeled
2 tsp salt
juice of ½ lemon
1 heaped tbsp brown sugar
2 tbsp peanut or sunflower oil

For the sticky rice
200g (7oz/1 cup) Thai long-grain sticky rice
a pinch of salt

For the peanut sauce
200g (7oz) salted, roasted peanuts
1 tbsp peanut or sunflower oil
2 tsp dark soy sauce
100ml (3½oz) coconut milk
2 tbsp dark brown sugar
juice of 1 lemon
optional: 2 tsp chilli flakes

For the cucumber salad
1 large cucumber
1 small red onion
1½ tbsp rice wine vinegar
1 tbsp sweet chilli sauce
1 tbsp freshly chopped coriander (cilantro)
½ tsp salt

1   First make the satay marinade by blitzing all the ingredients in a blender until finely ground. Setting aside 1 tablespoon for the peanut sauce, combine the chicken with the marinade, making sure it is well covered. Leave it to marinate in the fridge for 2 hours, or overnight.

2   As soon as you've put the chicken in the fridge, make a start on preparing the sticky rice. Tip the rice into a bowl and cover it with warm water so that the water comes about 5cm (2in) above the rice. Leave it to soak for 2 hours (or overnight).

3   To make the peanut sauce, grind the peanuts in a blender until they are fairly smooth – a few chunky bits are good. Heat the oil in a small saucepan over a low heat and add the reserved tablespoon of marinade. Let it cook for 1 minute, to bring out all the flavours. Add the rest of the peanut sauce ingredients and heat gently, stirring together. If you think it's too thick, add a little more coconut milk or some water. Give it a taste. If you like it sweeter, then add more sugar; if you want it sour, add more lemon; or for a spicier kick, add more chilli. Make it your own! Keep it in the fridge until needed.

4   About 30 minutes before you're ready to eat, bring a saucepan of water to a simmer. Drain the water from the rice and transfer the rice to a muslin cloth (or banana leaves). Sprinkle with the salt and then fold up the edges to seal. Steam over the pan of simmering water for 25 minutes, turning over the rice parcel halfway through so it cooks evenly. Keep an eye on the water levels in the pan so it doesn't dry out.

5   Meanwhile, get your griddle pan (or barbecue!) nice and hot. Thread the chicken on to skewers – I wear rubber gloves for this stage to stop my hands from getting stained yellow by the turmeric. Cook for 2 minutes on each side. If you have any leftover marinade, you can brush it on to the chicken as it cooks.

6   Just before serving, cut the cucumber and onion into chunky pieces and mix them together in a large bowl. Combine all the other salad ingredients in a smaller bowl, and then pour over the cucumber and onion. Give it a good stir. Serve the chicken with the rice and peanut sauce, and the salad on the side.

ROAST CHICKEN, BUTTERNUT SQUASH PURÉE, CAVOLO NERO AND POMEGRANATE JUS

Roast chicken is the ultimate in comfort food. Here, I have taken inspiration from my time living in Beirut and included pomegranate seeds in the gravy for a burst of freshness. Cavolo nero is Italian 'black cabbage', but kale or Savoy cabbage will work just as well.

Preparation time: 25 minutes
Cooking time: 1½ hours

SERVES 4

INGREDIENTS

1 x 1.7kg (3lb 12oz) whole chicken,
    washed inside and out
salt and pepper
1 lemon, halved
½ white onion, peeled
olive oil, to drizzle
300g (10½oz) cavolo nero
1 tbsp butter
salt and pepper

For the butternut squash purée

50g (2oz) butter
2 shallots, peeled and finely diced
800g (1lb 10oz) peeled and diced
    butternut squash
100ml (3½fl oz) vegetable stock
salt and pepper
freshly grated nutmeg, to taste

For the pomegranate jus

3 banana shallots, peeled and finely chopped
200ml (7fl oz) red wine
1 tbsp pomegranate molasses
500ml (14fl oz) reduced chicken stock
200g (7oz) pomegranate seeds

1   Preheat the oven to 220°C (425°F/gas 7). Pat the chicken dry with kitchen paper and season with salt and pepper. Stuff the cavity with the lemon halves and the onion. Place the chicken in a roasting dish and drizzle with a little oil. Roast in the oven for 15 minutes, then turn down the temperature to 190°C (375°F/gas 5) and roast the chicken for a further 1 hour 15 minutes, or until cooked through. To test if the chicken is ready, insert the tip of a knife into the thickest part of the breast meat near the leg; the juices should run clear.

2   While the chicken is cooking, make a start on the squash purée. Melt the butter in a large saucepan and cook the shallots for 2–3 minutes until soft. Add the squash and continue cooking for a couple of minutes. Pour over the stock, cover with a lid and simmer for 20–30 minutes, until the squash is tender. Season with salt, pepper and the nutmeg, and then blitz with a hand-held blender until smooth.

3   For the jus, put the shallots, wine and pomegranate molasses in a saucepan. Simmer over a low to medium heat for 15 minutes, until reduced by half. Add the stock and simmer for about 15 minutes, until reduced by half again. Stir through the pomegranate seeds.

4   Bring a saucepan of water to the boil, add the cavolo nero and cook for 5 minutes. Drain off the water but keep the cavolo nero in the pan. Add the butter and toss to coat, then season with salt and pepper.

5   When you are ready to serve, slice the chicken and serve with the squash purée, cavolo nero and drizzled with the jus.

DUCK WITH A PLUM, GINGER AND ORANGE SAUCE

Being half Chinese-Malaysian, I grew up enjoying many duck dishes at our family meals! This recipe uses a classic English Barbary duck breast, but it is served with an Asian-style sweet, salty and tangy sauce. I like to use Barbary duck breasts, as they are well known for their plump firm meat. Serve with a simple mustard mash and some blanched green beans.

Preparation time: 10 minutes
Cooking time: 15 minutes

SERVES 4

INGREDIENTS
4 Barbary duck breasts
salt and pepper
vegetable or sunflower oil, for greasing

For the sauce
4 tbsp light soy sauce
75g (2½oz/⅓ cup, plus 1 tbsp) caster sugar
1 tbsp freshly grated ginger
1 tbsp hoisin sauce
2 tbsp water
zest and juice of 1 orange
juice of 1 lime

1 Preheat the oven to 190°C (375°F/gas 5). Using a sharp knife, score the duck fat a few times. Pat the duck breasts dry with kitchen paper and season lightly with salt and pepper.

2 Brush a frying pan with a little oil and set over a high heat. When hot, place the duck breasts, skin-side down, in the pan and leave for 2 minutes to brown. Turn them over and leave for a further 2 minutes. Transfer the duck to a baking tray and cook in the oven for 6–7 minutes, depending on how you like your duck cooked and the size of the breasts. I like mine a little pink in the middle, but leave them in the oven for a couple of minutes longer if you like your duck more well done.

3 Meanwhile, make the sauce by simmering all the ingredients in a small pan for a couple of minutes until thickened slightly.

4 When the duck breasts are cooked to your liking, transfer them to a board and leave to rest for 3–5 minutes, before slicing. Serve the duck with some of the sauce spooned over the top.

SHREDDED ROAST DUCK WITH PUY LENTILS, POMEGRANATE AND MINT WITH HARISSA YOGHURT

This melt-in-the-mouth duck is full of flavour and it works really well alongside the vibrant nutritious lentil salad. Pomegranate seeds add a pop of juicy sweetness and the harissa yoghurt provides a nice bit of spice.

Preparation time: 25 minutes
Cooking time: 3 hoiurs

SERVES 4

INGREDIENTS

1 x 1.5kg (3lb 5oz) whole duck
salt and pepper
½ tsp hot chilli powder
½ tsp ground cinnamon
½ tsp ground cumin
250g (9oz/1 cup) Puy lentils
a bunch of mint leaves, very roughly chopped
a large ripe avocado, peeled and cut into pieces
50g (2oz) baby spinach
a bunch of spring onions (scallions), finely sliced
75g (3oz) pomegranate seeds
3 tsp harissa paste
6 tbsp natural yoghurt
3 tbsp pistachio nuts, roughly chopped

For the dressing
6 tbsp rapeseed oil
2 tbsp lemon juice
2 tbsp honey
1 tsp ground cinnamon
1 tsp ground cumin
2 tsp sumac
salt and pepper

1 Preheat the oven to 170°C (325°F/gas 3). Pat the duck dry with kitchen paper and sit it in a deep roasting tray. Mix together 1 teaspoon of salt with the chilli powder, cinnamon and cumin and rub all over the duck. Cook in the oven for 2½ hours, basting with the fat from the bottom of the roasting tray a couple of times.

2 Meanwhile, cook the lentils in boiling water for about 20 minutes, until tender. Drain and leave to cool.

3 When the duck is nearly cooked and the lentils have cooled, put the lentils, mint, avocado, spinach, spring onions and pomegranate seeds in a large bowl and lightly toss together.

4 Mix together the harissa and yoghurt. Season with salt and a twist of pepper and set aside.

5 Once the duck has cooked and cooled a little, use two forks to shred the meat and crispy skin.

6 In a small bowl, mix together the dressing ingredients and season with salt and pepper. Pour half over the salad and toss gently to combine and coat the salad in the dressing. Transfer to individual plates or one large serving platter for sharing.

7 Scatter the duck on top of the salad and finish by drizzling over the harissa yoghurt and sprinkling with pistachios. Offer any extra salad dressing separately.

Tip

If you haven't got time to roast the duck, use slices of smoked duck breast. You can even use pre-cooked Puy lentils.

PAN-FRIED PHEASANT WITH CELERIAC GRATIN, SPINACH AND CHARRED ROSCOFF ONIONS

Pheasant is a great meat: it is low in fat and usually completely organic and wild. It doesn't need a huge amount of cooking and it can very easily dry out, so keep this in mind as you cook it. The celeriac gratin is deeply savoury and the charred Roscoff onions are sweet and bitter all at once. The celeriac gratin is best made a day in advance.

Preparation time: 45 minutes, plus overnight to chill

Cooking time: 2 hours

INGREDIENTS
2 pheasant crowns
salt and pepper
25g (1oz) butter
olive oil, for drizzling
2 Roscoff onions (or red onions), peeled and halved

For the celeriac gratin
olive oil, for greasing
1 garlic clove, peeled and crushed with the flat of a knife
200ml (7fl oz) double (heavy) cream
25g (1oz) butter
a sprig of fresh thyme
salt and pepper
2 celeriacs, peeled and very thinly sliced using a mandolin

For the spinach purée
200g (7oz) spinach leaves
50ml (3fl oz) double (heavy) cream
1 tbsp butter
freshly grated nutmeg
salt and pepper

1 Preheat the oven to 170°C (325°F/gas 3). Lightly grease a 15cm x 15cm (6in x 6in) ovenproof dish.

2 Put the garlic, cream, butter and thyme in a saucepan and warm through over a medium heat. Season with salt and pepper. Place the celeriac slices in a bowl and pour over the hot cream. Leave until cool enough to handle then start to layer them in the ovenproof dish. Press the slices down, so they are compact, and continue until you reach the top of the dish. Pour over the cream and cover with foil. Bake in the oven for 40 minutes, then remove the foil and cook for a further 30 minutes. Remove from the oven and leave to cool (ideally overnight). Press down on the top to make it really dense. When cool, remove from the dish and cut into strips or wedges.

3 To cook the pheasant, preheat the oven to 200°C (400°F/gas 6). Season the pheasant with plenty of salt and pepper. Melt the butter in an ovenproof frying pan and, when hot, place the pheasant breast-side down in the pan. Cook for 5–10 minutes to seal the meat then transfer the pan to the oven along with the gratin for 20 minutes to warm through. Remove from the oven and let the pheasant rest, breast-side down while you cook the onions. Keep the oven on.

4 Heat a griddle pan over a medium heat and drizzle the onion halves with oil. Place the onions, flat-side down on the griddle pan and cook for 5–8 minutes – they should be quite dark. Pop them in the oven for about 10 minutes to finish cooking. Remove from the oven and leave to cool a little, then separate the layers of each onion into petals.

5 While the onions are cooking and cooling, make the purée. Blanch the spinach in boiling water for 1 minute, then drain and refresh in a bowl of ice-cold water. Heat the cream, butter and nutmeg in a small saucepan, then drain the spinach and add it to the cream mixture. Blitz to a fine purée using a hand-held blender and season to taste with more nutmeg and some salt and pepper.

6 Serve the pheasant with the spinach purée, slices of the warm celeriac gratin and the onion petals.

MEAT

LEMON, PARMESAN AND PINE NUT CRUSTED PORK WITH APPLE AND FENNEL COLESLAW

This recipe is simple, versatile and delicious, especially if you add some skinny fries on the side! Chicken or veal both work really well as alternatives to pork. Instead of rosemary, you can use sage, oregano or thyme, and the pine nuts can be swapped with pretty much any nuts, such as cashews, hazelnuts, Brazil nuts or walnuts.

Preparation time: 40 minutes
Cooking time: 6 minutes

SERVES 4

INGREDIENTS

4 pork loin steaks
110g (4oz) crustless white bread, torn into
    rough pieces
finely grated zest of 1 lemon
50g (2oz) finely grated Parmesan cheese
50g (2oz/¼ cup) pine nuts
2 sprigs of rosemary, leaves picked
1 tsp fennel seeds, lightly crushed
salt and freshly ground pepper
3 tbsp plain (all-purpose) flour
2 eggs, beaten
olive oil, for shallow frying
lemon zest and wedges, to serve

For the coleslaw

1 Granny Smith apple
1 tbsp lemon juice
½ fennel (approx. 110g/4oz)
¼ red cabbage (approx. 225g/8oz)
125g (4½oz) radishes
2 shallots, peeled
125g (4½oz) crème fraîche
50g (2oz) natural yoghurt
2 tsp Dijon mustard
2 tsp cider vinegar
1 tsp celery salt
salt and pepper

1 To make the coleslaw, remove the core from the apple and cut the apple into matchsticks. Put into a large bowl and toss in the lemon juice. Very finely slice or shred the fennel, cabbage, radishes and shallots either using a very sharp knife and a steady hand, a mandolin or the slicer blade on a food processor. Add to the apple and toss together.

2 Mix together the crème fraîche, yoghurt, mustard, vinegar and celery salt. Season with a good twist of pepper and mix thoroughly into the vegetables. Season to taste.

3 Trim the fat from the pork loins then, one at a time, place between two pieces of greaseproof paper. Bash with a rolling pin or meat mallet to flatten them until they are about 5mm (¼in) thick.

4 Put the bread in the bowl of a food processor with the lemon zest, Parmesan, pine nuts, rosemary, fennel seeds and a pinch each of salt and freshly ground pepper. Blitz until well combined and it has formed a fine breadcrumb consistency. Tip into a shallow bowl. Place the flour on a plate and the beaten eggs in a separate shallow bowl.

5 Heat about 1cm (½in) of oil in 2 large frying pans. Season the pork escalope with salt and pepper and dust with the flour. Dip into the egg then press into the crumbs, coating evenly. Cook in the hot oil for 2–3 minutes on each side, until golden and crunchy.

6 Serve immediately with lemon zest scattered over the top, lemon wedges, and a spoonful of the apple and fennel coleslaw.

SLOW-ROASTED PORK BELLY WITH SWEET AND SOUR APPLES AND POTATO PURÉE

This is a dish that I make for dinner parties all the time. The pork is so tender that it falls apart in your mouth, while the salty crackling adds a crunchy contrast. The apple sauce is sweet and sour all in one go, cutting through the fat and bringing out the meaty flavour.

Preparation time: 25 minutes
Cooking time: 3½ hours

SERVES 4

INGREDIENTS

800g–1kg (1¾lb–2lb 3oz) piece of free-range, off-the-bone pork belly, skin scored
2 onions, peeled and sliced into thick rings
1 tsp fennel seeds
2 tsp sea salt
100ml (3½fl oz) white wine

For the jus
1 shallot, peeled and finely chopped
1 carrot, peeled and finely chopped
1 stick of celery, finely chopped
100g (3½oz) bacon lardons, finely sliced
1 tbsp olive oil
50g (2oz) butter
1 garlic clove, peeled and finely chopped
150ml (5fl oz) red wine
500ml (16fl oz) good-quality chicken stock

For the potato purée
1kg (2lb 3oz) Maris Piper potatoes
100–120g (3½–4oz) butter
a dash of milk or double (heavy) cream
salt and white pepper

For the sweet and sour apples
1 Granny Smith apple
40g (1½oz) caster sugar
2 tbsp white wine vinegar
a pinch of sea salt

1 Preheat the oven to 220°C (425°F/gas 7). Pat dry the pork belly skin with kitchen paper. Arrange the onion rings in the bottom of a roasting tray

2 Lightly crush the fennel seeds and salt in a pestle and mortar. Rub this into the skin of the pork, then place the pork on top of the onions. Roast for 30 minutes, or until the skin turns golden brown and starts to bubble and crackle. Reduce the oven temperature to 160°C (320°F/gas 2) and continue to cook for 1½ hours. At this point, open the oven door and carefully add the wine to the roasting tray. Cook for a further 1½ hours.

3 When the pork has about 45 minutes of cooking time left, make the jus. Gently fry the shallot, carrot, celery and bacon in a pan with the oil and half the butter for about 10 minutes, until golden brown and sticky. Add the garlic and cook for a further minute. Deglaze the pan with the red wine and simmer gently until reduced by three-quarters. Stir in the chicken stock and simmer gently for 30 minutes, until it has reduced by half and is thick and syrupy. Just before serving, remove from the heat and whisk in the remaining butter.

4 Meanwhile, peel the potatoes and cut into large chunks. Cook in a large pan of salted boiling water for 10–15 minutes, until tender. Drain, then return them to the hot pan to dry out for 5 minutes before passing through a ricer (or mashing until very smooth). Gradually mix in the butter, adding a little milk or cream to help loosen the mixture. Once you have a smooth and soft consistency, season with salt and pepper, then cover to keep warm.

5 To make the sweet and sour apples, peel and cut them into 1cm (½in) dice. Sprinkle the sugar on the bottom of a non-stick frying pan and place over a medium heat. As the sugar starts to melt and turns golden brown, swirl the pan but don't be tempted to stir it! Once it has melted and is a caramel colour, remove from the heat and carefully add the apple pieces. Add the vinegar and return to the heat. Stir until the sugar has dissolved, then simmer for 1 minute. Season with a little salt and remove from the heat.

6 Once the pork is cooked and the meat is tender, remove from the oven. Place the pork on a board and rest for 10 minutes, while you finish the jus. Place the roasting tray over a low heat and add a little water or chicken stock. Cook for 3–4 minutes and use a spoon to scrape off any caramelized bits from the bottom of the pan. Add the pan juices to your jus and pass through a fine sieve. Cut the pork into squares and serve on top of the smooth potatoes and the apples. Spoon the jus around the edge.

LAMB RUMP WITH GOAT'S CHEESE GNOCCHI

This is a wonderful springtime dish. Spring is a great time for produce: artichokes and asparagus are the king and queen of vegetables, and lamb rump works very well with them. The gnocchi is very simple to make, and can be made a day in advance.

Preparation time: 50 minutes
Cooking time: 1 hour 15 minutes

SERVES 4

INGREDIENTS

1 globe artichoke
12 asparagus spears, woody ends removed
200g (7oz) peas
4 x 180g (6oz) lamb rump steaks
salt and pepper
50g (2oz) butter
1 tbsp olive oil
a small handful of chopped mint

For the gnocchi

500g (1lb 2oz) floury potatoes, such as
    King Edwards, scrubbed
1 egg
150g (5oz/1¼ cup) plain (all-purpose) flour,
    plus extra for dusting
50g (2oz) hard goat's cheese (Berkswell is
    great here), grated
1 tbsp olive oil
50g (2oz) butter
salt and black pepper

1 Preheat the oven to 200°C (400°F/gas 6). Arrange the potatoes on a baking tray and bake in the oven for 1 hour, or until cooked through.

2 While the potatoes are cooking, prepare the artichoke. Bring a large pan of water to the boil. Slice off most of the crown, about 3cm (1in) from where the stem meets the base. Pull off any smaller leaves towards the base and on the stem. Run a sharp knife around the edge of the artichoke to remove any tough skin and leaves. Cut off any excess stem, leaving up to 3cm (1in). Peel off the tough outside layer of the stem with a vegetable peeler. Take a spoon and scoop out the fuzzy 'choke' of the artichoke. Plunge into the boiling water and cook for about 30 minutes until tender. Refresh under cold running water and set aside.

3 Blanch the asparagus and peas in a pan of boiling water for 2 minutes, then drain and refresh under cold running water and set aside.

4 Heat an ovenproof frying pan over a high heat. Season the lamb with salt and pepper and cook for 1 minute on each side to seal, then remove from the heat and set aside.

5 Remove the potatoes from the oven (but keep the oven on), cut them in half and scoop out the flesh into a bowl. Keeping the potato covered with a tea towel so it doesn't dry out, pass it through a sieve or potato ricer into a large bowl. Add the egg and flour and mix in the goat's cheese to form a soft dough – don't overwork it, as it will become gluey and tough.

6 Bring a large saucepan of lightly salted water to a rapid boil. Roll out the dough on a lightly floured surface to form sausage shapes roughly 2.5cm (1in) wide and 40cm (15in) long. Cut into 2.5cm (1in) pieces and transfer them to a floured plate. Add half the gnocchi to the pan of boiling water and cook for 5 minutes. Remove with a slotted spoon and drain. Repeat with the remaining gnocchi.

7 Heat the oil in a frying pan and fry the gnocchi until they are just starting to brown on each side. Add the butter and season with salt and pepper.

8 Meanwhile, pop the lamb in the oven and cook for a further 5 minutes, or until cooked through but still pink inside. Remove from the oven and leave to rest while you reheat the veg. Heat the butter and oil in a frying pan and add the peas, artichoke wedges and the asparagus spears. Warm through, then stir in the mint.

9 When everything is ready, slice the lamb and serve with vegetables and gnocchi.

MOROCCAN LAMB, PISTACHIO AND PRESERVED LEMON KEFTA TAGINE WITH MINTED COUSCOUS

Bring a little of the Middle East to your table with this superb aromatic tagine. The beauty of this dish is that you can make it a day in advance and the flavours just get better and better. I also like to prepare the couscous ahead of time and simply heat it through and add the mint just before serving.

Preparation time: 40 minutes
Cooking time: 45 minutes

SERVES 4

INGREDIENTS

For the kefta (meatballs)
500g (1lb 2oz) minced (ground) lamb
2 onions, peeled and finely chopped
50g (2oz/½ cup) pistachio nuts, chopped
1 tsp ground cumin
1 tsp ground cinnamon
¼ tsp cayenne pepper
a small bunch of coriander (cilantro), chopped
3 preserved lemons
salt and pepper
2 tbsp olive oil
25g (1oz) fresh ginger, peeled and grated
   or finely chopped
1 red chilli, finely chopped
a pinch of saffron
300ml (11fl oz) hot lamb stock
1 tbsp tomato purée
50g (2oz) pitted black Kalamata olives, halved

For the couscous
250g (9oz/1⅓ cup) couscous
300ml (11fl oz) hot vegetable or lamb stock
1 tbsp olive oil
a small bunch of mint, chopped

To serve
2 tbsp pomegranate seeds
2 tbsp pistachio nuts, roughly chopped
a handful roughly chopped coriander (cilantro)

1   To make the kefta, place the lamb mince in a large bowl with one of the chopped onions, the pistachios, dried spices and chopped coriander. Quarter and remove the flesh from one of the preserved lemons. Finely chop the lemon peel and add to the lamb mince. Season well with salt and pepper, then thoroughly mix everything together with your hands. To check for seasoning, heat a drop of oil in a small frying pan, and fry a small lamb 'burger' for a minute on each side. Have a taste and add more salt to the mix if required. Shape into walnut-sized balls, making roughly 20 kefta (meatballs).

2   Heat the oil in a large casserole, then add the kefta and brown all over. Remove with a slotted spoon and set aside on a plate before adding the remaining onion, and the ginger, chilli and saffron to the casserole. Sauté for about 5 minutes until the onion has softened and is starting to colour. Add the stock, tomato purée and olives and bring to the boil. Cut the remaining 2 preserved lemons into wedges and add to the casserole along with the kefta. Reduce the heat, cover with a lid and cook for 20 minutes, turning the meatballs a couple of times. Remove the lid and cook without the lid for a further 10 minutes until the liquid has reduced and thickened slightly.

3   Put the couscous in a large bowl and pour over the hot stock and oil. Stir well and cover with a lid or piece of cling film. Leave for 5 minutes then run a fork through to separate the couscous grains, making it light and fluffy. Stir in the chopped mint.

4   Serve the couscous scattered with pomegranate seeds, and finish the tagine with a scattering of pistachios and chopped coriander.

Tip

Any minced meat can be used for this dish and if you don't have preserved lemons, use the finely grated zest of one fresh lemon in the meatballs and one lemon cut into wedges in the sauce.

AMI-YAKI BEEF WITH A FRESH HERB SALAD

I love grilled meats and the Japanese do them very well. Ami-yaki translates as 'net grilling', and it describes the traditional method of grilling meat, fish or vegetables on a wire net over a high heat. The first restaurant I worked in served many amazing grilled dishes, so this one is inspired by them. It is perfect cooked on the barbecue.

Preparation time: 20 minutes, plus 30 minutes marinating

Cooking time: 5 minutes

SERVES 2

INGREDIENTS

2 x 180g (6oz) fillet steaks, each 5cm (2in) thick

For the marinade

100ml (3½oz) soy sauce
3 tbsp sugar
½ tbsp sesame oil
2 tbsp toasted sesame seeds
2 spring onions (scallions), finely chopped
1 heaped tbsp finely grated fresh ginger
juice of 1 lemon
a pinch of pepper

For the salad

1½ tbsp olive oil
1 tbsp lemon juice
a pinch of salt and pepper
approx. 100g (3½oz) mixed green leaves
1 tbsp freshly chopped coriander (cilantro) leaves
1 tbsp freshly chopped mint leaves
1 tbsp freshly chopped basil leaves

1 Heat the soy, sugar and 3 tablespoons of water in a saucepan over a low heat for a couple of minutes, until the sugar has dissolved. Remove from the heat, leave to cool for 10 minutes and then stir in the rest of the marinade ingredients.

2 Slice each fillet steak into 3 pieces about 1.5cm (5/8in) wide. Coat in the marinade and let sit for 30 minutes (no need to put it in the fridge).

3 Get your griddle pan (or barbecue) nice and hot. Just before you cook the beef, prepare the salad by mixing the oil, lemon juice and the salt and pepper together in a large bowl. Add the salad leaves and herbs and toss together.

4 Cook the beef for 40–60 seconds on each side, depending how you like your steak cooked. I like to use any leftover marinade as extra sauce, so while your steak is cooking, simply pour the marinade into a pan and warm it through for a minute. Serve the steak with the salad and any sauce drizzled on top.

"Caroline's cooking is full of flavour and this beef ami-yaki is full of those fantastic umami notes – totally gorgeous!"

STEAK AND CHIPS

When asked what their last meal would be, most people say 'steak and chips!' There are so many different cuts of steak, each with a different taste and texture, but my personal favourite is a rib-eye, cooked medium-rare and served with a large dollop of English mustard and a flavoured butter, a grilled portobello mushroom and some tomatoes . . . and a large side of chips, of course!

Preparation time: 2 minutes,
plus 5 minutes resting

Cooking time: 5 minutes

SERVES 4

INGREDIENTS

steak of your choice, approx 2cm (³/₄in) thick
olive oil
salt and pepper

1 Remove your steaks from the fridge about 30 minutes before you plan to cook them so that they can come up to room temperature.

2 Heat a griddle or a non-stick frying pan over a high heat until it is super hot, but not quite smoking.

3 Rub or brush the steaks with a drop of oil and season with salt and a little pepper. Cook for about 1½ minutes on one side, then flip them over and cook for a further minute or so. Carry on flipping the steaks every minute, until cooked to your liking. As a guide, a medium-rare 2cm- (³/₄ in-) thick steak will take about 5 minutes to cook.

4 If there is a piece of fat running along the edge of your steak, use some tongs to hold the steak up vertically in the pan to brown the fat.

5 Remove the steaks from the pan, place them on a warm plate and leave to rest for a good few minutes (this is essential) before serving with a couple of slices of flavoured butter on top or your chosen sauce.

TGK CHIPS

Preparation time: 10–15 minutes
Cooking time: 15–30 minutes,
depending on the size of your fryer

SERVES 4

INGREDIENTS

8 large floury potatoes (such as Maris Piper, King Edward or Desiree), peeled and cut into chips (as thick or thin as you like!)
sunflower, groundnut or vegetable oil, for deep-frying
sea salt

1 Boil the chipped potatoes in a large pan of water for 5–8 minutes (depending on their thickness), until just starting to soften. Drain well and pat dry.

2 Pour the oil into a large saucepan or your deep fryer and heat to 180°C (350°F). If you don't have a kitchen thermometer, you can check the oil is hot enough by dropping in a small cube of bread. It should fizz and turn brown within about 40 seconds.

3 Carefully lower in the chips – you may need to do this in batches. It's important not to overcrowd the pan as this will decrease the temperature of the oil and you might end up with soggy chips! Cook the chips for 2–3 minutes or until golden and crispy. Shake off any excess fat and season with salt before serving.

"On the next page you'll find some sauces and flavoured butters to try out with your steak – one from each of us and all completely delicious."

PORCINI, ROASTED GARLIC AND THYME BUTTER

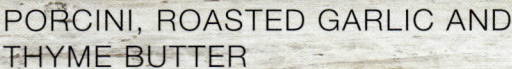

INGREDIENTS

1 bulb of garlic
olive oil
25g (1oz) dried porcini
mushrooms
1½ tsp fresh thyme
leaves
150g (5oz) good-quality
salted butter, softened
freshly ground black
pepper

1 Preheat the oven to 200°C (400°F/ gas 6). Cut off the stalk from the bulb of garlic, just low enough to remove the tips from the cloves. Drizzle with oil and wrap in a double layer of foil. Place on a baking tray and roast for 45 minutes or until it feels soft when lightly pressed. Unwrap and leave to cool.

2 Meanwhile, soak the mushrooms in hot water for 30 minutes. Drain well, squeeze out any excess water, then chop finely. Place the mushrooms in a mixing bowl and add the rest of the ingredients. Squeeze the garlic flesh out of their skins into the bowl and mix together.

3 Spoon the flavoured butter on to a double layer of cling film and roll it up to form a sausage shape about 3cm (1¼in) in diameter. Twist the ends to seal like a cracker. Leave to set in the fridge. The butter will keep for a couple of days or freeze it and cut off slices as needed.

CHIMICHURRI

INGREDIENTS

25g (1 oz) flat-leaf parsley
25g (1 oz) fresh coriander
3 tbsp fresh basil leaves
120ml (4fl oz) olive oil,
plus 1 tbsp to serve
2 small shallots, peeled
2 serrano peppers or
jalapeños
3 or 4 garlic cloves, peeled
2 tbsp cider vinegar (or
red wine vinegar)
juice of ½ lime
½ tsp salt

1 This is super easy! Simply put everything in a food processor and whizz until it has a fairly fine consistency. It doesn't have to be completely smooth, bits of herb are perfectly OK – I like mine quite chunky!

2 Rub a couple of tablespoons of the sauce into your steak and leave it to marinate for 2 hours. If you're short on time, even half an hour will make a difference to the taste.

3 Once you've cooked your steak, leave it to rest and then slice it. Mix a couple of tablespoons of the sauce with an extra tablespoon of oil and drizzle it over the top of the steak. Serve any extra sauce on the side. It will keep for up to a week in the fridge but it's best to make it fresh.

WATERCRESS AND HORSERADISH BÉARNAISE

INGREDIENTS

1 tbsp olive oil
1 shallot, peeled and
    finely chopped
1 tbsp vinegar (any type)
4 egg yolks
300g (10 oz) slightly
    warm clarified butter
    (or you can use
    melted butter)
4 tbsp freshly grated
    horseradish
4 tbsp chopped
    watercress
sea salt and pepper
a squeeze of lemon juice

1 Heat the oil in a small pan over a low to medium heat. Fry the shallot until soft and translucent. Add the vinegar and cook until it has reduced to about a teaspoon.

2 Bring a small saucepan of water to the boil and set a heatproof bowl on top (make sure the bottom of the bowl doesn't actually touch the hot water). Place the egg yolks and the shallot reduction in the bowl and whisk until light and fluffy. Slowly add the warm butter, whisking as you go, until you have a thick and glossy sauce.

3 Stir in the grated horseradish, chopped watercress, and season with salt, lots of pepper and, finally, a squeeze of lemon. Serve with a perfectly cooked steak.

RED WINE AND SHALLOT BUTTER

INGREDIENTS

250g (9 oz) salted butter,
    softened
3 large banana shallots,
    peeled and
    finely chopped
1 garlic clove, peeled
    and finely chopped
1 tbsp fresh thyme
    leaves
400ml (13fl oz)
    medium-bodied red
    wine (such as Merlot
    or Shiraz)

1 Melt 50g (2oz) of the butter in a frying pan over a medium to low heat. Add the shallots, garlic and thyme and cook for 10 minutes until soft and translucent but not coloured.

2 Pour in the wine and simmer until reduced (you should have around a tablespoon of liquid left in the pan). Remove from the heat, scrape into a bowl and leave to cool a little. Whisk in the remaining butter.

3 Spoon the flavoured butter on to a double layer of cling film and roll it up to form a sausage shape about 3cm (1¼in) in diameter, then twist the ends to seal it like a cracker. Pop it into the fridge to set. Use up the butter within a couple of days or keep it in the freezer and slice off discs whenever you need it.

TGK BURGER WITH MELTED GRUYÈRE, TRUFFLE MAYO AND CRISP ONION RINGS

For somewhere as GORGEOUS as THE GORGEOUS KITCHEN, only the best ingredients for our burgers will suffice. So, here comes a humdinger: semi-brioche buns, truffle-scented mayonnaise, red onion marmalade, melted Gruyère, onions rings and smoked bacon. This is a seriously moreish burger. This recipe makes more TGK onion marmalade than you need for the burgers, but it will keep in sterilized jars for up to a month and it goes with everything!

Preparation time: 50 minutes, plus 2–3½ hours resting

Cooking time: 1 hour 10 minutes

INGREDIENTS

For the semi-brioche buns

3 tbsp warmed milk

1 tsp caster sugar

2 tsp dried yeast

450g (1lb/4¼ cups) strong bread flour, plus extra for dusting

1 tsp salt

2 tbsp butter

1 egg, plus 1 egg yolk

olive oil

sesame seeds, for sprinkling

For the TGK onion marmalade

2 tbsp olive oil

1kg (2lb 3oz) red onions, peeled and finely sliced

125g (4½oz/⅔ cup) dark brown sugar

150ml (5fl oz) red wine vinegar

90ml (3fl oz) Ribena (or blackcurrant cordial)

50ml (2fl oz) port

salt and pepper

1   To make the buns, mix together the milk with 250ml (8fl oz) warm water, the sugar and yeast in a small bowl. Leave to one side for 5 minutes. Sift the flour and salt into a large bowl and then rub in the butter with your fingertips until the mixture resembles fine breadcrumbs. Whisk the whole egg into the yeast mixture. Make a well in the middle of the flour mixture, then pour in the yeast mixture and knead together, to form a rough, sticky dough. Turn out the dough on to a lightly floured work surface and knead for 10 minutes, or until the dough is smooth and elastic. Put the dough in a clean, oiled bowl, and lightly oil the dough. Cover with a damp, clean tea towel and leave in a warm, draught-free place for 1–2 hours, or until the dough has doubled in size.

2   Lightly dust a baking tray with flour. Knock the air out of the dough, turn out on to a lightly floured work surface and knead again for 5 minutes. Divide the dough into 8 pieces and place them on the baking tray at least 5cm (2in) apart. Cover with a tea towel and leave in a warm place for 1½ hours. The buns need to be a lot bigger before they are cooked, so don't be tempted to rush this stage, otherwise they will be tough.

3   Preheat the oven to 180°C (350°F/gas 4). Fill an ovenproof dish with water and place it in the bottom of the oven. This will create moisture as the buns cook, giving the crust a lovely chewy texture. Brush the buns with the egg yolk and sprinkle with the sesame seeds. Bake for 30–35 minutes until golden brown, then transfer to a wire rack to cool.

4   While the buns are cooking and cooling, get on with the rest of the burger. First make the onion marmalade. Heat the oil in a large pan over a medium heat. Add the onions and cook gently for about 15 minutes, or until soft and translucent. Add the sugar and stir well. Cook for 5 minutes before adding the vinegar, Ribena and port. Mix together and then simmer gently for 45 minutes, stirring occasionally until it has reduced and thickened. Add a pinch of salt and pepper, then spoon into sterilized jars.

(recipe continued overleaf)

INGREDIENTS (continued)

For the truffle mayonnaise
100g (3½oz) good-quality mayonnaise
1 tsp chopped truffle paste from a jar
1 tsp Dijon mustard
½ tsp truffle oil

For the burgers
200g (7oz) beef shoulder, coarsely minced
250g (9oz) chuck steak, coarsely minced
250g (9oz) hanger steak, coarsely minced
200g (7oz) bone marrow
salt and pepper

For the onion rings
200g (7oz/12/3 cups) self-raising flour, plus
    extra for dusting
100g (3½oz/¾ cup, plus 2 tbsp) cornflour
200ml (7fl oz) sparkling water
salt and pepper
1 litre (32fl oz) vegetable oil, for deep-frying
2 Roscoff onions (or red onions), peeled and
    sliced into 5mm (¼in) rings

To serve
½ tbsp olive oil
2 rashers of smoked streaky bacon,
    cut into lardons
4 slices of Gruyère cheese

5 While the onion marmalade is cooking, mix together the ingredients for the truffle mayonnaise and chill in the fridge until needed.

6 Combine the ingredients for the burgers in a bowl, season well and bring the mixture together with your hands. Shape into 4 patties.

7 Next make the batter for the onion rings by mixing the two flours together with the sparkling water. Season with salt and pepper and set to one side.

8 Heat the oil for the bacon in a small pan and fry the bacon pieces for a few minutes until crisp. Drain on kitchen paper and set aside.

9 Preheat the grill. Get your griddle pan on a high heat. Cook the burgers for about 5 minutes on each side, or until cooked to your liking.

10 Meanwhile, pour the oil for the onion rings into a large, deep saucepan, wok or a deep fryer. Heat to 170–185°C (340–360°F). If you don't have a kitchen thermometer, you can drizzle a little batter into the oil and if it immediately sizzles to the top it's hot enough. Dust the onion rings in flour and then dip them into the batter. Carefully lower them into the hot oil and cook for 4–5 minutes, until golden brown. Drain on kitchen paper.

11 When the burgers are cooked, scatter over some of the crispy bacon, top each one with a slice of cheese and pop them under the grill to melt the cheese.

12 To assemble the burger, cut the buns in half and lightly toast them. Spread a teaspoon of onion marmalade on the base and a large teaspoon of the truffle mayonnaise on the top bun. Place a burger on the bottom bun and top with the onion rings and the bun lids.

Tip

If you're going to save time and buy your burgers from a butcher, make sure you get really good-quality ones with a mixture of skirt steak and bone marrow.

PASTA & RISOTTO

WILD MUSHROOM, GARLIC AND ROSEMARY LASAGNE

This lasagne was inspired by a simple pasta dish I learned at the first restaurant I worked in. Wild mushrooms are packed full of flavour and make a hearty and delicious filling for this creamy and satisfying lasagne. Serve with a simple green salad.

Preparation time: 20 minutes
Cooking time: 40 minutes

INGREDIENTS

2 tbsp butter
3 tbsp olive oil
3 large shallots, peeled and finely chopped
3 garlic cloves, peeled and finely chopped
1 tbsp finely chopped fresh rosemary leaves
450g (1lb) mixed wild mushrooms,
    roughly sliced
15g (½oz) dried porcini mushrooms,
    rehydrated (retain the soaking water)
80ml (3fl oz) white wine
3 tbsp double (heavy) cream
salt and pepper
200g (7oz) ricotta cheese
200g (7oz) cream cheese
250g (9oz) fresh lasagne sheets
2 tbsp freshly grated Parmesan cheese

1   Preheat the oven to 180°C (350°F/gas 4). Melt the butter and 2 tablespoons of the oil in a large pan over a medium to high heat. Add the shallots, garlic and rosemary and fry for 2 minutes until soft. Add all the mushrooms (chop any larger soaked ones if you think they are too big) and cook for 2–3 minutes, until soft. Stir in the wine and let it bubble for 30 seconds, then stir in 2 tablespoons of the reserved mushroom soaking liquid and the cream. Season with a pinch each of salt and pepper, remove from the heat and leave to one side.

2   Mix together the ricotta and cream cheese in a small bowl. Now you can start layering up the lasagne! Start with a layer of lasagne on the base of a 18cm x 20cm (7in x 8in) ovenproof dish. Top with about one-third of the mushroom mixture, then dot with a little of the ricotta and cream cheese mix – you need to keep back about 3 tablespoons for the topping so don't use a lot here. Repeat the process until you have used up all the lasagne sheets and mushrooms, finishing with a layer of lasagne. Mix the rest of the ricotta and cream cheese with the Parmesan and remaining 1 tablespoon of oil and spread it over the top.

3   Cover the dish with foil and bake for 15 minutes, then remove the foil and let cook for another 15 minutes, until the top browns.

Tip

Depending on how cheesy you like it, you can scatter some mozzarella chunks over the top just before cooking.

LIGHTLY SPICED BUTTERNUT SQUASH AND RICOTTA RAVIOLI

Ravioli are great fun to make at home and you can experiment with all sorts of fillings. I usually make a big batch and then freeze them; they can be cooked straight from the freezer and are great for last-minute suppers.

Preparation time: 30 minutes, plus 30 minutes to 1 hour to chill

Cooking time: 1 hour 10 minutes

SERVES 4

INGREDIENTS

For the pasta dough
400g (14oz/3⅓ cups) Type 00 flour, plus extra for dusting

4 whole eggs, plus 1 egg yolk, whisked together

a handful of semolina, for dusting

For the filling
600g (1lb 3oz) butternut squash

50g (2oz) butter

2 banana shallots, peeled and finely chopped

½ tsp dried chilli flakes

½ tsp ground cinnamon

100g (3½oz) ricotta cheese

50g (2oz) finely grated Parmesan cheese, plus extra to serve

salt and pepper

For the sage butter
150g (5oz) unsalted butter

a bunch of sage

1 First make the filling for the ravioli. Preheat the oven to 190°C (375°F/gas 5). Halve the butternut squash and lay it on a baking tray, cover in foil and roast for about 40–60 minutes. Remove from the oven and scoop out the flesh into a bowl.

2 While the squash is cooking, make the pasta dough. Place the flour in a large mixing bowl and make a well in the centre. Pour in half the whisked egg and mix into a dough using your hands, adding the remainder of the egg, as needed – you may not need it all. The pasta should come together but it shouldn't stick to your hands; add a little more flour if you think it needs it. Turn out the dough on to a lightly floured surface and knead for a few minutes until smooth. Cover with cling film and chill in the fridge for 30 minutes to 1 hour.

3 Melt the butter in a frying pan and cook the shallots until translucent. Add the chilli and cinnamon and then remove from the heat and add the squash, ricotta and Parmesan. Mash together, season with salt and pepper and leave to cool.

4 When ready to assemble, divide the dough into quarters and put one piece through a pasta machine, starting at the widest setting and working down to the final setting. Lay out the strip of pasta flat on a floured work surface, cover with a clean tea towel, and then repeat with the rest of the dough.

5 Lay one pasta sheet on a large chopping board. Place heaped teaspoons of the filling all over the sheet at 3cm (1½in) intervals. Brush around the mounds of filling with a little water, then place a second sheet of pasta on the top. Carefully press down around the mounds of filling to seal the sheets together. Using a sharp knife or a ravioli cutter, cut into squares. Place the ravioli on a baking tray dusted with semolina. Repeat with the rest of the pasta sheets and filling.

6 Bring a large saucepan of lightly salted water to the boil. When it is boiling rapidly, carefully drop in the ravioli and cook for 8 minutes until al dente.

7 Meanwhile, melt the butter in a large frying pan over a medium to low heat. Add the sage leaves and cook until foaming.

8 When the pasta is cooked, drain in a colander, reserving a little of the cooking water. Gently toss the pasta with a little of the water in the pan. Season with salt and pepper and serve immediately, drizzled with the sage butter and with plenty of grated Parmesan on top.

PRAWN, CHILLI AND ROCKET LINGUINE WITH PANGRITATA

One thing we can learn from Italian cooking is that some of the best dishes are pure simplicity. This recipe is one such dish. The flavour of the prawns is allowed to stand out and be the star, while rocket is used for something other than a salad.

Preparation time: 15 minutes
Cooking time: 25 minutes

SERVES 4

INGREDIENTS

450g (1lb) linguine
2 tbsp olive oil, plus a little extra to drizzle
2 garlic cloves, peeled and finely sliced
1 red chilli, de-seeded and finely chopped
400g (14oz) peeled and de-veined raw
    king prawns
125ml (4fl oz) white wine
300g (10½oz) cherry tomatoes, halved
salt and pepper
2 large handfuls of rocket (arugula) leaves
a squeeze of lemon juice

For the pangritata

4 slices of ciabatta, torn into rough pieces
1 garlic clove, peeled
2 tbsp olive oil
salt

1 First make the pangritata by placing the bread, garlic and oil in a blender. Blitz until you have medium-sized breadcrumbs – you don't want it to turn into a powder.

2 Heat a dry frying pan over a high heat, tip in the breadcrumbs and fry, stirring often, for 2–3 minutes, until golden brown. Season with salt and leave to one side.

3 Get a large pan of salted water on to boil and set a large frying pan over a medium heat. Add the pasta to the water and cook for a minute less than the packet instructions suggest.

4 Meanwhile, heat the oil in the frying pan and add the garlic and chilli. Cook for a minute before adding the prawns. Fry for a minute and then pour in the wine. Bubble until reduced by about half, then add the tomatoes and simmer for 2–3 minutes until slightly thickened. Season with salt and pepper.

5 Drain the pasta, reserving a little of the cooking water. Add the pasta to the sauce and mix together to coat. If it starts to become thick and claggy, add a little of the reserved pasta cooking water to loosen the sauce.

6 Stir in the rocket, allowing it to wilt slightly. Check the seasoning and divide between 4 warm pasta bowls. Drizzle with a little oil, sprinkle over the warm pangritata and finish with a squeeze of lemon juice.

SWEET SAUSAGE, TOMATO AND FENNEL RIGATONI

You can't go wrong by serving a good bowl of comforting pasta and this is such a straightforward recipe, you'll find yourself making it on a regular basis. The key to getting the best out of the sauce is to buy good-quality sausages with a high meat content. Don't go for anything too flavoured, as you will overpower the rest of the sauce. And make sure you add a good scattering of Parmesan – it would be a crime not to.

Preparation time: 10 minutes
Cooking time: 35 minutes

SERVES 4

INGREDIENTS

2 tbsp olive oil
1 medium fennel, core removed and
  finely sliced
400–450g (14oz–1lb) thick pork sausages
2 plump garlic cloves, peeled and chopped
1 tsp fennel seeds, crushed
¼ tsp dried chilli flakes
200ml (8fl oz) medium dry white wine
1 tbsp tomato purée
400g (14oz) tin of chopped tomatoes
1 tsp caster sugar
1 tsp balsamic vinegar
salt and pepper
½ a bunch of basil leaves, torn
  into pieces
400g (14oz) rigatoni (or penne or any
  large pasta shapes)
freshly grated Parmesan cheese, to serve

1 Heat the oil in a non-stick frying pan over a low heat and gently fry the fennel for about 10 minutes, until it is soft but not coloured.

2 Meanwhile, remove the sausages from their skins and break the meat into small pieces. Add the sausage pieces, garlic, crushed fennel seeds and chilli flakes to the pan and fry for about 8 minutes, breaking the sausage meat down with a wooden spoon into smaller pieces. Once the sausage meat starts to turn golden and become sticky, pour in the wine and let it bubble until it has reduced by half. Stir in the tomato purée, tinned tomatoes, sugar and vinegar and season with salt and pepper. Partially cover the pan with a lid and simmer for 10 minutes. Stir in the basil and continue to cook without a lid for a further 5 minutes, until the sauce is rich and thick. Check the seasoning.

3 While the sauce is cooking, cook the pasta in boiling salted water for a minute less than the packet instructions suggest, and then drain.

4 Stir the cooked pasta into the sauce and cook together for about 1 minute, then serve in bowls with plenty of Parmesan scattered over the top.

HAM HOCK AND CARAMELIZED PEARL ONION RISOTTO

Cooking your ham hocks from scratch means that this recipe takes a long time. To speed it up, you can always buy your ham ready cooked. It's a very satisfying dish, so you don't need anything more than a lightly dressed leafy green salad to go with it.

Preparation time: 20 minutes
Cooking time: 2½ hours

INGREDIENTS

2 tbsp butter
1 onion, peeled and finely chopped
2 garlic cloves, peeled and finely chopped
1 tbsp freshly chopped thyme
300g (10½oz/1⅔ cups) Arborio rice
salt and pepper
125ml (4fl oz) white wine
500ml (16fl oz) hot chicken stock
1 tbsp freshly chopped fat-leaf parsley, plus
    extra to serve
50g (2oz) freshly grated Parmesan cheese
2 tbsp double (heavy) cream

For the pearl onions
20 pearl onions, peeled
3 tbsp caster sugar

For the ham hocks
2 tbsp sunflower oil
3 ham hocks, to yield 250g (9oz) meat
    once cooked
1 carrot, roughly chopped
1 stick of celery, roughly chopped
1 onion, peeled and roughly chopped
1 bay leaf
½ glass of white wine

1   To cook the ham hocks, heat the oil in a large saucepan with a lid over a medium to high heat. Add the hams and turn them every minute or so, until browned all over. Drain off some of the oil, then add the chopped vegetables and bay leaf and cook for a couple of minutes. Pour in the white wine and let it bubble for 30 seconds, then pour over enough water to cover the hams. Place a lid on the pan, turn down the heat to low and simmer gently for 2 hours – or you can transfer the pan to an oven preheated to 150°C (300°F/gas 2) to slow cook (make sure the saucepan is ovenproof!). Cook until the meat is tender and falling apart.

2   When the hams are cooked, lift them out and leave to one side to cool a little. Reserve 200ml (7fl oz) of the stock for the risotto. Once the meat has cooled, shred it or cut it into chunks.

3   Boil the pearl onions in a saucepan of water for 3 minutes. Drain off the water, but keep the onions in the pan. Add the sugar and cook over a medium to high heat for 2–3 minutes, moving the onions around so they get evenly coated in the sugar and start to caramelize. Once the onions are browned all over, tip them into a bowl ready to serve with your risotto.

4   Melt the butter in a large saucepan and cook the onion, garlic and thyme over a low heat for 5 minutes – be careful not to let them brown. Add the rice and salt and stir well, making sure the rice is coated in the buttery onions. Pour in the wine and keep stirring until has been absorbed. Next, gradually add the hot chicken stock a ladle at a time, stirring continuously until all the stock has been absorbed before adding another ladle. Keep going until all the chicken stock and the reserved ham hock stock have been absorbed. (If you don't have the ham hock stock, just use a little more chicken stock or water). Making a risotto can't be rushed, so relax and enjoy the process with a glass of wine! It will take about 25 minutes. Check the rice is cooked – it should be soft but with a firm bite and the risotto should be lovely and thick and creamy.

5   When it is cooked, stir in the parsley, chopped ham, Parmesan and cream. Check the seasoning and add a pinch of pepper and extra salt, if needed. Serve topped with a few pearl onions and garnish with an extra sprinkling of parsley.

SUMMER VEGETABLE RISOTTO

Many people shy away from making a risotto when entertaining because it requires a lot of standing at the cooker and stirring. There is, however, a brilliant restaurant technique that means you can make a head start the day before. All you need to do is par-boil the rice first, then chill it. It can be kept covered in the fridge for up to 24 hours. So, the next time you have people over, try this delicious risotto, packed full of tasty summer vegetables with an extra flavour burst from the herby, lemony gremolata – and never miss out on the gossip again.

Preparation time: 25 minutes
Cooking time: 20 minutes

SERVES 4

INGREDIENTS

300g (11oz/1½ cup) carnaroli or Arborio rice
flaked sea salt and freshly ground black pepper
200g (7oz) asparagus spears, cut into
    approx. 4cm (1½in) pieces
200g (7oz) shelled fresh or frozen broad
    beans, defrosted if frozen
110g (4oz) fresh or frozen peas, defrosted
    if frozen
2 tbsp olive oil
25g (1oz) butter
1 large or 2 small shallots, peeled and
    finely chopped
150ml (5fl oz) white wine
a bunch of spring onions (scallions),
    finely sliced
75g (3oz) finely grated Parmesan cheese,
    plus shavings for serving
extra virgin olive oil, for drizzling

For the gremolata

2 tbsp freshly chopped basil
2 tbsp freshly chopped chives
1 tbsp freshly chopped mint
finely grated zest of 1 lemon

1 Start off by cooking the rice in a large pan of boiling salted water for 8 minutes. Drain well and tip on to a baking tray. Chill in the fridge until you are ready to finish the risotto.

2 Bring 1 litre (32fl oz) of water to the boil with a good pinch of salt. Add the asparagus and, if the beans and peas are fresh, add them here too. If you are using defrosted frozen ones, keep to one side. Cook for 2 minutes.

3 Using a slotted spoon, remove the vegetables from the pan (keeping the cooking water) and pop them straight into a bowl of iced water to stop them from cooking. Once they are cold, drain and set aside. For a better flavour and colour to the finished dish, pop the broad beans out of their skins, revealing their vibrant green flesh. The prepared vegetables can be kept cold in the fridge for a good few hours before finishing the risotto. The vegetable-flavoured cooking water from the vegetables is now your stock to make the risotto, so don't throw it away.

4 When you are ready to finish the risotto, gently heat the oil and half of the butter in a large saucepan. When the butter is bubbling, add the shallot and gently cook until softened. Meanwhile, place the reserved stock over a medium heat and bring to a simmer.

5 To make the gremolata, simply mix together the herbs and lemon zest.

6 Pour the wine into the shallot pan and cook until it has reduced by half. Stir in the chilled rice and a ladle of the hot stock. When the stock has been absorbed, continue adding the stock a ladle at a time, waiting until it has been absorbed before you add the next. It will only take about 6 minutes until the rice is cooked and has a shiny glaze. You may not need all the stock.

7 Add the asparagus, broad beans, peas and spring onions and stir until they are heated through. Add a little extra stock if needed. Mix in the Parmesan, remaining butter and herb gremolata. Have a taste and season with salt and pepper. Cover with a lid and leave to sit for a couple of minutes before spooning on to plates or into bowls. A scattering of Parmesan shavings, a twist of black pepper and a drizzle of oil will finish off your masterpiece beautifully.

CLAM, MUSSEL, SQUID AND FREGOLA STEW

Fregola is a type of pasta from Sardinia – lovely little globes that soak up flavour. Here, I have cooked it in a rich tomato, saffron and garlic sauce, and finished off the dish with some fresh seafood. Gremolata is traditionally sprinkled on meat dishes, but I think it provides a wonderful lift to this seafood stew.

Preparation time: 20 minutes
Cooking time: 1 hour

SERVES 4

INGREDIENTS

50ml (2fl oz) extra virgin olive oil, plus
  extra to drizzle
2 banana shallots, peeled and sliced
3 garlic cloves, peeled and sliced
a pinch of dried chilli flakes
a large pinch of saffron
a splash of Pernod
50ml (2fl oz) white wine
500ml (16fl oz) chopped tomatoes
1.5l fish stock
salt and pepper
a pinch of caster sugar
300g (10½oz) fregola
200g (7oz) clams, cleaned
200g (7oz) mussels, cleaned and
  de-bearded (discard any that are open)
150g (5oz) squid rings

For the gremolata
a handful of chopped flat-leaf parsley
a handful of chopped tarragon
zest of 2 lemons
1 garlic clove, peeled and finely chopped
1 tbsp fresh breadcrumbs

1 Heat the oil in a large shallow saucepan over a medium heat. Add the shallots, garlic and chilli flakes and cook for a couple of minutes until translucent. Add the saffron, Pernod and wine and cook for 2 minutes, then add the tomatoes and stock. Season with salt and pepper, add the sugar and then leave to simmer for 20 minutes so all the flavours can combine, stirring occasionally to stop the sauce sticking.

2 Stir the fregola into the sauce and cook for about 20 minutes, until al dente.

3 Add the clams, mussels and squid rings and cook for a further 5–8 minutes, until all the clams and mussels have opened.

4 Meanwhile, mix together the ingredients for the gremolata.

5 To serve, pile the stew into bowls, sprinkle some gremolata over the top and drizzle with a little oil.

SPELT, WILD MUSHROOM AND CHICKEN 'RISOTTO'

This is a great alternative to a traditional risotto. The spelt adds a delicious nuttiness to the dish. It is also quicker to cook, so it's perfect for when you don't want to be a slave to the hob.

Preparation time: 20 minutes
Cooking time: 50 minutes

SERVES 4

INGREDIENTS

800ml (26fl oz) hot good-quality
   chicken stock
6 chicken thighs, de-boned, trimmed and
   cut into thirds
250g (9oz/1 ¼ cup) pearled spelt
10g (1/3oz) dried porcini mushrooms
3 tbsp olive oil
90g (3fl oz) butter
1 onion, peeled and finely diced
1 tbsp thyme leaves
150g (5oz) chestnut mushrooms, finely sliced
2 garlic cloves, peeled and very finely
   chopped
100ml (3½fl oz) medium dry white wine
100g (3½oz) mixed wild mushrooms
salt and pepper
1 tbsp finely chopped tarragon
30g (1oz) grated Parmesan cheese

1   Pour 300ml (10fl oz) chicken stock into a small pan, add the chicken pieces and simmer very gently for 30 minutes, until the meat is tender.

2   Meanwhile, soak the spelt in cold water for 20 minutes. Place the dried mushrooms in a bowl, cover with boiling water and leave for 20 minutes.

3   Heat 2 tablespoons of the oil and 1 tablespoon of the butter in a large frying pan over a medium heat. Gently fry the onion and thyme until the onion is soft and translucent, then add the chestnut mushrooms and continue to cook for 3 minutes before stirring in the garlic.

4   Drain the porcini mushrooms, reserving the soaking liquid, and roughly chop them.

5   Drain the spelt and stir into the onions with the chopped porcini mushrooms, making sure everything is well coated in the butter. After 2 minutes, deglaze the pan with the wine, scraping off anything that is stuck to the bottom. Simmer gently until the wine has almost completely evaporated. Stir in the reserved liquid from the porcini mushrooms.

6   Gradually start to add the rest of the chicken stock, a ladle at a time, stirring continuously until all the stock has been absorbed before adding another ladle.

7   Check on the chicken and when tender and cooked through, remove from the stock and set aside. Turn up the heat to medium high and reduce the stock until thick and syrupy.

8   While the stock is reducing and the spelt is cooking, heat 20g (¾oz) butter in a large frying pan and fry the wild mushrooms for 2 minutes. Season with salt and pepper and then stir in the tarragon and set aside.

9   Heat 20g (¾oz) butter and the remaining tablespoon of oil in a clean frying pan and fry the chicken on one side for 2 minutes until golden brown.

10   Once all the stock has been absorbed and the spelt is al dente, remove from the heat and stir in the remaining butter and the Parmesan. Remove from the heat and leave with the lid on for 2 minutes.

11   Serve in warm bowls, scattered with the cooked wild mushroom and topped with the chicken. Finish with a drizzle of the reduced stock.

PUDDINGS
& BAKING

BITTER CHOCOLATE MOUSSE WITH SALTED CARAMEL AND SHORTBREAD DIPPERS

Dense, rich chocolate mousse and sweet salty caramel is a match made in heaven. Serve with homemade shortbread biscuits on the side to dip into the mousse and the whole dish is to die for. It's like a deconstructed millionaire's shortbread biscuit, but, dare I say it . . . better.

Preparation time: 40 minutes, plus 2 hours chilling
Cooking time: 35–40 minutes

SERVES 4–6

INGREDIENTS

For the shortbread dippers
115g (4oz) unsalted butter, at room temperature
40g (1½oz/¼ cup) caster sugar, plus extra for sprinkling
½ tsp vanilla extract
150g (5oz/1 cup) plain (all-purpose) flour, plus extra for dusting
a pinch of salt
40g (1½oz/¼ cup) fine semolina

For the salted caramel sauce
50g (2oz/¼ cup) soft brown sugar
40g (1½oz) unsalted butter
25g (1oz) golden syrup
75ml (3fl oz) double (heavy) cream
½ tsp flaked sea salt

For the mousse
150g (5oz) dark (70% cocoa) chocolate, broken into small pieces
1 tsp instant coffee granules mixed with 1 tbsp hot water and left to cool
2 large eggs, separated
2 tbsp caster sugar
150ml (5fl oz) double (heavy) cream

1. To make the shortbread, beat together the butter, sugar and vanilla until it is light in colour and consistency. Mix in the flour, salt and semolina and finish by bringing it together with your hands to form a soft pliable dough. Wrap in cling film and place in the fridge for about 30 minutes. Preheat the oven to 160°C (320°F/gas 2).

2. Meanwhile, to make the salted caramel sauce, put the sugar, butter and golden syrup in a saucepan over a low heat and stir until the butter has melted. Bring to a simmer for roughly 2 minutes, so the sauce thickens, swirling the pan a couple of times. Add the cream and salt and simmer for a further minute. Remove from the heat, transfer to a jug and cool to room temperature.

3. Once the shortbread dough has chilled, dust your work surface with a little flour and roll out the dough until it is about 1cm (½in) thick. Using a sharp knife, cut into slim fingers, approximately 6cm x 5mm–1 cm (2½in x ¼–½in), re-rolling any trimmings as you go (you should be able to make around 24). Arrange them on a baking tray lined with baking parchment and cook in the oven for 35–40 minutes until they are just starting to turn lightly golden. As soon as they come out of the oven, sprinkle with a little caster sugar and cool on a wire rack.

4. To make the mousse, gently melt the chocolate in a large heatproof bowl set over a pan of simmering water. Make sure the bottom of the bowl doesn't actually touch the hot water. Remove from the heat and allow to cool for 5 minutes. Mix in the coffee and egg yolks and set aside.

5. Whisk the egg whites in a large bowl until they hold firm peaks when the whisk is lifted. Whisk in the sugar until the whites are glossy and firm.

6. In a separate bowl, whisk the cream until thick. Fold half of the cream into the chocolate followed by half of the egg whites. Repeat using the remaining half of the cream and then the egg whites. Fold together gently until you have a rich, even chocolate colour throughout.

7. Spoon half of the chocolate mousse into small dishes, glasses or coffee cups. Add a layer of the caramel (warming it very gently in the microwave or on a low heat if it has firmed up too much) and top with the remaining mousse. Spoon and swirl more caramel over the top and place in the fridge to chill for a couple of hours before serving with the shortbread fingers to dip.

RHUBARB AND CUSTARD TRIFLES

You can't beat rhubarb and custard! It reminds me of the sweets I used to have as a child. The ginger in these mini trifles gives this pudding an extra kick.

Preparation time: 15 minutes, plus cooling time

Cooking time: 15 minutes

INGREDIENTS

300g (10½oz) gingerbread, cut into 6 slices about 2cm (¾in) thick
150g (5oz) crystallized ginger in syrup, chopped into strips

For the custard

500ml (16fl oz) whole (full-cream) milk
1 vanilla pod
125g (4½oz/⅔ cup) caster sugar
6 egg yolks
1½ tbsp plain (all-purpose) flour
2 tsp cornflour
200ml (7fl oz) double (heavy) cream

For the rhubarb compote

300g (10½oz) rhubarb, cut into 2.5cm (1in) pieces
100g (3½oz/½ cup) caster sugar

1 First make the custard by heating the milk and vanilla together gently in a saucepan over a low heat. Whisk the sugar and egg yolks together in a bowl, then add the flours and whisk again to combine. Slowly pour the milk on to the egg mixture, whisking continuously. Pour the mixture back into the hot saucepan and set over a medium heat. Heat it to just before boiling point, stirring all the time until it thickens and coats the back of the spoon. Be careful not to let the custard boil as it will curdle. Remove from the heat and cover the surface with a layer of cling film to stop a skin forming. Leave to cool for 10–15 minutes.

2 While the custard is cooling, make the rhubarb compote. Put the rhubarb and the sugar in a saucepan with a splash of water. Bring to the boil and cook for a few minutes until tender, then remove from the heat and leave to cool.

3 Whip the cream and fold it into the cooled custard.

4 To assemble the trifles, cut out a circle from each slice of gingerbread to fit your serving glasses. Scatter a little crystallized ginger in the bottom of each glass and top with a slice of gingerbread. Spoon over the custard and finish with the rhubarb compote. Chill until ready to serve.

COCONUT PANNA COTTA WITH BLUEBERRY COMPOTE AND TOASTED COCONUT FLAKES

This is one of my go-to recipes when I've got my best pals round for dinner. It can be prepared a day or two in advance without compromising on flavour. It's deliciously sweet but not too heavy, and the juicy, tangy blueberry compote is A M A Z I N G served with the silky smooth and creamy panna cotta.

Preparation time: 20 minutes, plus 3 hours to set (or overnight)
Cooking time: 15 minutes

MAKES 4

INGREDIENTS

4 gelatin leaves
400ml (14fl oz) coconut milk
25g (1oz/¼ cup) desiccated coconut
200ml (7fl oz) single (light) cream
110g (4oz/1 cup) caster sugar
150g (5oz) natural yoghurt
a small handful of dried coconut flakes, to serve

For the compote

150g (5oz) blueberries
2 tbsp caster sugar
2 tsp lemon juice
½ tsp arrowroot mixed with 1 tsp cold water

1   Soak the gelatin leaves in a bowl of cold water for about 5 minutes to soften

2   Place the coconut milk, desiccated coconut and cream in a saucepan over a medium heat and stir in the sugar. Gently bring to the boil, stirring occasionally then remove from the heat. Squeeze any excess water from the gelatin then stir it into the cream mixture until dissolved. Leave for about 30 minutes to cool completely.

3   Stir in the yoghurt until smooth, using a balloon whisk if necessary, then strain through a sieve into a large jug, discarding the desiccated coconut. Pour into individual cups, glasses or dishes and leave to set in the fridge for 3 hours or overnight if you have the time.

4   To make the compote, place the blueberries in a saucepan with the sugar and lemon juice. Bring to a simmer over a medium heat, stirring occasionally. Cook for about 1 minute until some of the blueberries burst open giving you a deep blue juice in the pan. Stir in the arrowroot and keep stirring until it thickens slightly. Remove from the heat and leave to cool to room temperature.

5   Heat a frying pan over a medium heat and add the coconut flakes. Toss around in the pan for 2–3 minutes, until slightly golden. Remove from the heat and let cool.

6   To serve, spoon the blueberry compote on top of the panna cottas and sprinkle with toasted coconut.

Tip

Blueberries are ideal to use when in abundance. However, when they are not in season I like serving the panna cotta with poached rhubarb flavoured with orange zest, roasted plums flavoured with star anise or cinnamon, or diced fresh mango mixed with passion fruit and lime zest.

WHITE CHOCOLATE AND PEACH CHEESECAKES WITH MACADAMIA NUT BRITTLE

These are lovely, sweet, creamy, little hand-held delights. The white chocolate really enriches the flavour and the peaches are subtly aromatic and delicate. I make them in muffin tins and then they are ready to grab and go.

Preparation time: 25 minutes, plus 30 minutes to cool

Cooking time: 15 minutes

INGREDIENTS

For the peach compote
300g (10½oz) peaches, chopped
100g (3½oz/½ cup) caster sugar

For the biscuit base
150g (5oz) digestive biscuits, crushed
75g (2½oz) butter, melted
a pinch of salt

For the cheesecake mix
250g (9oz) cream cheese
75g (2½oz/⅓ cup, plus 1 tbsp) caster sugar
2 tsp cornflour
100ml (3½fl oz) double (heavy) cream
1 large egg
½ vanilla pod, seeds scraped
100g (3½oz) white chocolate, melted and
   then cooled

For the nut brittle
100g (3½oz/½ cup) caster sugar
100g (3½oz) macadamia nuts

1 Preheat the oven to 160°C (320°F/gas 2). Line a 10-cup muffin tray with foil cases.

2 First make the peach compote. Put the peaches, sugar and a little water in a saucepan and bring to the boil. Simmer for a few minutes, until you have a thick compote. Remove from the heat and leave to cool completely.

3 Meanwhile, mix the crushed biscuits with the melted butter. Pack a dessertspoon of the biscuit mixture into the bottom of each case in the muffin tray, then place in the fridge while you make the creamy topping.

4 Beat together the cream cheese, sugar and cornflour. Add the cream, egg and scraped vanilla pod and whisk well. Finally, stir in the cooled melted chocolate until evenly mixed through. Pour the mixture on top of each of the biscuit bases until it reaches about 5mm (¼in) below the top. Then put them back in the fridge for about 15 minutes to set.

5 Meanwhile, make the Macadamia nut brittle, by putting the sugar and 50ml (2fl oz) water in a saucepan and bringing to the boil. Simmer until it forms a rich, thick golden brown caramel. Lay out the nuts on a baking tray lined with baking parchment and pour the cameral over the top. Leave to cool and then crush into small pieces with a rolling pin.

6 Spoon some of the compote on top of each cheesecake and sprinkle with a little nut brittle.

ELDERFLOWER AND SUMMER BERRY JELLY WITH LEMON ICE CREAM

Sparkling elderflower is always my drink of choice at a barbecue or wedding when I am the designated driver. It tastes like summer in a glass. This is my grown-up take on that childhood classic, jelly and ice cream. I sometimes serve it with a tuile biscuit on top.

Preparation time: 40 minutes, plus 6 hours to set

Cooking time: 5 minutes

SERVES 4

INGREDIENTS

4 gelatin leaves
200ml (7fl oz) sparking wine or prosecco
50g (2oz/¼ cup) caster sugar
200ml (7fl oz) sparkling elderflower drink
4 tbsp elderflower cordial
150g (5oz) raspberries
100g (3½oz) blueberries

For the ice cream

6 egg yolks
100g (3½oz/½ cup) caster sugar
zest and juice of 2 lemons
500ml (16fl oz) double (heavy) cream
200g (7oz) lemon curd

1 Make the jelly by soaking the gelatin in a bowl of cold water for 10 minutes, until soft.

2 Pour half the sparkling wine into a small saucepan over a medium heat and add the sugar. Once the sugar has dissolved and the wine is simmering, remove the gelatin from its soaking water and squeeze out any excess water. Remove the pan from the heat and stir in the gelatin. Once it has dissolved, pour in the sparkling elderflower drink, the elderflower cordial and the remaining bubbles and stir well.

3 Pour the jelly mixture into 4 serving glasses, top with the berries then leave to set in the fridge for at least 6 hours.

4 Meanwhile, make the ice cream. Place the egg yolks and sugar in a bowl set over a pan of just simmering water (make sure the bottom of the bowl doesn't actually touch the hot water). Whisk with an electric beater until doubled in volume, pale in colour and it forms ribbons when you lift out the whisk. Remove from the heat and whisk in the lemon zest and juice. Continue whisking until cool.

5 Lightly whip the cream, then fold the lemon curd into the cream. Fold into the egg mixture. Either place in an ice cream machine and churn until soft-set, or scrape into a container and freeze for 2 hours, then remove and beat well with a fork. Beat every hour until set (about 6 hours). Remove the ice cream from the freezer 10 minutes before serving, to soften slightly.

AMARETTO TIRAMISU

Tiramisu is my absolute favourite pudding. It covers all the bases in my book: bitterness from the coffee, sweetness from the sugar and alcohol, and creaminess from the mascarpone. It is perfect served in a large bowl to share or, as I've done here, in individual glasses for a smart dinner party dessert.

Preparation time: 15 minutes, plus 2 hours to chill (or overnight)

SERVES 4

INGREDIENTS
250g (9oz) mascarpone cheese
5 tbsp Amaretto liqueur
3 egg yolks
50g (2oz/¼ cup) caster sugar
200ml (7fl oz) strong cold coffee
16 sponge finger biscuits
2 tbsp flaked almonds
1 tbsp icing (powdered) sugar
2 tbsp cocoa powder

1 Mix together the mascarpone and 3 tablespoons of the Amaretto.

2 Put the egg yolks and caster sugar in a separate bowl. Using an electric hand-mixer, beat them together until pale and fluffy, then fold in the mascarpone mixture.

3 Mix together the coffee and the remaining 2 tablespoons of Amaretto in a shallow dish. Quickly dip 4 of the biscuits into the mixture and place in the bottom of 4 individual glasses – you may need to break them up a bit so that they fit snugly.

4 Spoon over a little of the mascarpone mixture to cover the biscuit. Quickly dip 3 more biscuits into the coffee mixture then pop these in one of the glasses on top of the mascarpone mixture. Repeat with the other 3 glasses. Finally spoon over the rest of the mascarpone mixture. Chill in the fridge for 2 hours, or overnight.

5 While they are chilling, heat a dry frying pan over a high heat. Add the flaked almonds then sprinkle over the icing sugar. Use a wooden spoon to mix the two together constantly. When they have turned golden brown, tip them out on to a piece of baking parchment. Leave to cool.

6 When ready to serve, dust the tiramisus with cocoa powder then sprinkle with a few of the caramelized flaked almonds.

LEMON MERINGUE CUPCAKES

I'm a bit lemon crazy and as lemon meringue pie is one of my favorite desserts, I thought I'd recreate it here as a cupcake. Light sponge with a zesty lemon curd centre and soft meringue on top makes this a little bit of cupcake heaven.

Preparation time: 40 minutes, plus 20 minutes cooling

Cooking time: 40 minutes

MAKES 12

INGREDIENTS

200g (7oz/1 cup) caster sugar
115g (3oz) unsalted butter
2 tsp lemon zest
2 large eggs, lightly beaten
225g (8oz/1¾ cup, plus 2 tbsp)
    self-raising flour
salt
120ml (4fl oz) milk
1 tbsp lemon juice
1 tsp vanilla extract

For the lemon curd filling

75g (2½oz) unsalted butter
190g (6⅔oz/1 cup) caster sugar
2 large eggs, plus 2 egg yolks
160ml (5½fl oz) lemon juice
2 heaped tsp grated lemon zest

For the meringue topping

3 large egg whites
75g (2½oz/⅔ cup) caster sugar

1. To make the lemon curd, use an electric whisk to beat the butter and sugar until fluffy. Add the eggs and egg yolks, beat well and then pour in the lemon juice and zest and beat again. It will look curdled but that is fine. Tip into a small saucepan and place on a low heat. Keep stirring until it looks smooth, then increase the heat to medium and cook for 5–7 minutes, without letting it boil, until it thickens. Transfer to a bowl, place a piece of cling film on top (to stop a skin from forming) and leave to cool.

2. While the lemon curd is cooling, make your cake batter. Preheat the oven to 180°C (350°F/gas 4). Using an electric whisk, beat the sugar, butter and lemon zest until light and fluffy. Add the beaten egg, a little at a time, making sure it is completely mixed in before adding any more.

3. Sift half the flour and a pinch of salt into the bowl and beat into the mixture with the milk, lemon juice and vanilla. Sift in the remaining flour and beat until you have a smooth batter.

4. Line a 12-cup muffin tray with paper cases and spoon the batter into the cups until they are about two-thirds full. Cook in the oven for 12–15 minutes or until the cakes are lightly golden and they spring back when you press the sponge with your finger. (Or insert a small skewer in and if it comes out clean, it's done!) Remove from the oven and transfer the cakes to a wire rack to cool completely.

5. When the cakes have cooled, use a teaspoon to scoop out a round hole from the middle of the top of each cake. (I usually eat the cutout pieces as I go!) This is to make room for the lemon curd – just be careful the holes aren't too big or else the cakes may break. Fill the holes with a good dollop of lemon curd.

6. Next make the meringue topping. Preheat the oven to 160°C (320°F/gas 2). Whisk the egg whites until they form stiff peaks, then gently sprinkle the sugar over the top while continuing to whisk until glossy, stiff peaks form.

7. Using either a piping bag or a spoon, swirl the meringue on top of the cakes. Pop them in the oven for 15 minutes so the meringue cooks and sets. If you have a blowtorch you can also lightly scorch the outside once they have cooked. Leave them to cool before serving and eating the same day.

"Cooking for others is a great pleasure for us, and it's amazing to think how many people we'll be feeding every day at The Gorgeous Kitchen."

CARROT CAKE WITH CLEMENTINE FROSTING AND CANDIED PECANS

There is something about carrot cake that makes it feel like it's less of a naughty treat. This recipe uses wholemeal flour, raisins and plenty of clementine zest, giving you even more reasons to have an extra slice! The flavours only get better with time, so don't worry if you don't quite finish it off in one go as it will keep for several days.

Preparation time: 45 minutes
Cooking time: 25 minutes

MAKES 12–16 SLICES

INGREDIENTS

200ml (7fl oz), plus 2 tbsp rapeseed or sunflower oil
125g (4½oz/⅔ cup) soft light brown sugar
3 medium eggs, lightly beaten
110g (4oz) golden syrup
225g (8oz/1¾ cups, plus 2 tbsp) wholemeal self-raising flour
1½ tsp ground cinnamon
½ tsp ground allspice
½ tsp ground ginger
1½ tsp bicarbonate of soda (baking soda)
275g (10oz) peeled and finely grated carrots
110g (4oz/½ cup) sultanas
40g (1½oz/½ cup) desiccated coconut

For the candied pecans

75g (3oz/½ cup) pecans, roughly chopped
50g (2oz/¼ cup) caster sugar
½ tsp ground allspice

For the frosting

75g (3oz) unsalted butter, at room temperature
150g (5oz) cream cheese
325g (13oz/3¼ cup) icing (powdered) sugar, sifted
finely grated zest of 4 clementines
1 tbsp runny orange blossom honey

1 Preheat the oven to 180°C (320°F/gas 2). Lightly brush 2 x 20cm (8in) round cake tins with a little oil and line the bases with a circle of baking parchment.

2 In a large bowl or using an electric mixer, whisk together the oil, sugar, eggs and golden syrup until totally combined. Mix in all of the remaining cake ingredients and divide between the prepared tins. Bake in the oven for 20–25 minutes until nicely risen and firm but springy when lightly pressed. Insert a skewer into the centre of the cakes and if it comes out clean, they are cooked. Leave to cool in the tins for 10 minutes before turning out on to a wire rack to cool completely.

3 Meanwhile, to make the candied pecans, toss together the pecans, sugar and allspice in a wide non-stick pan. Place over a high heat, tossing frequently, until the sugar has caramelized and the nuts are well coated. Transfer to a tray lined with baking parchment. Leave to cool and harden for about 10 minutes, then lightly break into small pieces.

4 For the frosting, beat the butter with an electric mixer until smooth. Add the cream cheese and beat for another minute or so. Add half the icing sugar and mix together on a low speed, then add the remaining icing sugar and mix until it is a light creamy texture. Add the clementine zest and honey and give it a final mix. Keep in a cool place until needed.

5 To make up the cake, sandwich the cakes together with some of the frosting then use the rest to ice the top. Scatter the candied pecans over the top.

BLACKBERRY CRUMBLE CAKE

This recipe was inspired by a tray bake one of my aunties brought to a family function when I was young. Tasting it for the first time is still a vivid memory: it was halfway between a pudding and a cake, and I immediately had to ask her for the recipe! This recipe is how it has evolved over the years.

Preparation time: 25 minutes
Cooking time: 45–50 minutes

MAKES 10–12 SLICES

INGREDIENTS

180g (6oz) butter, at room temperature,
    plus extra for greasing
200g (7oz/1 cup) caster sugar
50g (2oz/¼ cup) brown sugar
3 large eggs
1 tsp vanilla extract
2 tsp baking powder
185g (6½oz/1½ cups) plain (all-purpose) flour
2 tbsp milk
250g fresh or frozen blackberries

For the topping

100g (3½oz/¾ cup, plus 2 tbsp) plain
    (all-purpose) flour
2 tbsp firmly packed brown sugar
3 tbsp butter
1 tbsp cornflour
¼ tsp cinnamon
2 tbsp chopped pecans

1   Preheat the oven 180°C (350°F/gas 4). Grease a deep-sided 24cm x 30cm (9½in x 12in) cake tin or baking tray with a little butter and line it with baking parchment.

2   Start by making the crumble topping. Put the flour, sugar and butter in a bowl and use your fingertips to rub it until it forms big breadcrumbs. Add the cornflour, cinnamon and pecans and toss through. Set aside.

3   Next make the cake batter. Beat the butter and sugars together until light and fluffy. Beat in the eggs, one at a time, and then mix in the vanilla. Sift the baking powder and half the flour into the bowl, and then beat in the milk and the remaining flour. Once you have a smooth batter, tip it into your cake tin.

4   Smooth over the surface of the batter with a spoon and sprinkle the blackberries on top. Scatter over the crumble topping and then cook in the oven for 45–50 minutes. You can test whether the cake is cooked by inserting a skewer into the middle; if it comes out clean, it is cooked – you might get a bit of blackberry on there, but that's OK. Leave the cake to cool in the tin, then turn it out and serve. As with all cakes, this is best eaten on the day you make it but will keep for a couple of days in an airtight container.

Tip

Switch up the fruit depending on seasons: use apples, raspberries, cherries, plums or whatever you fancy. Use the same quantity, but make sure there aren't any stones!

ULTIMATE CHOCOLATE CAKE

This recipe has been in our family for years. I used to make it for friends at school for their birthdays and it always went down a treat. It is only now that I can reveal the secret to its deliciously moist texture: mayonnaise! Try it; it's amazing. The mayonnaise will also help it keep for longer – not that you'll need it to.

Preparation time: 20 minutes, plus 1 hour to cool

Cooking time: 35 minutes

MAKES 8–10 SLICES

INGREDIENTS

280g (10oz/2⅓ cups) self-raising flour
1½ tsp baking powder
4 tbsp cocoa powder, sifted
225g (8oz/1 cup, plus 2tbsp) caster sugar
1 tsp vanilla extract
200g (7oz) mayonnaise
40g (1½oz) milk chocolate, flaked, to serve

For the chocolate icing

125g (4½oz) butter
4 tbsp cocoa powder, sieved
3 tbsp evaporated milk
225g (8oz/2¼ cups) icing (powdered) sugar, sifted

1   Preheat the oven to 180°C (350°F/gas 4). Line the base and side of a deep 22cm (8½in) round tin with baking parchment.

2   Put the flour, baking powder, cocoa powder and caster sugar in a large bowl and stir together. Spoon the mayonnaise into the bowl and add the vanilla but do not mix anything together at this stage, however tempting it is!

3   Measure out 225ml (7½fl oz) boiling water straight from the kettle, then pour it into the bowl and mix everything together until smooth.

4   Pour the mixture into the prepared cake tin and bake for 30 minutes, or until a skewer inserted into the centre comes out clean. Transfer to a wire rack to cool for 5 minutes before removing from the tin and leaving to cool completely.

5   When the cake has cooled, make the icing. Put the butter, cocoa powder and evaporated milk in a small saucepan and allow them to melt together over a low heat. Remove from the heat and stir in the icing sugar. Mix everything together until smooth and completely incorporated. Leave to cool for 10 minutes until it is not quite so runny. Placing a piece of cling film directly on the surface will stop a 'skin' forming.

6   Pour the cooled icing on top of the cake. Use a spatula to spread the icing towards the edge of the cake and allow it to run down the sides. Smooth the icing over the whole cake and either leave it with a smooth finish or add strokes of texture. Scatter over the flaked chocolate then pop the cake in the fridge to set the icing for 10 minutes before serving.

Tip

This is amazing popped in the microwave for 20 seconds and served with ice cream or crème fraîche.

RHUBARB & GINGER MULE

MAKES 8

INGREDIENTS
400g (14oz) rhubarb,
    chopped into pieces
40g (1½oz) peeled and
    finely chopped
    fresh ginger
300g (11oz/1½ cups)
    caster sugar
400ml (10fl oz) vodka
8 tsp fresh lime juice
1 litre chilled good-quality
    ginger beer
ice, fresh mint leaves and
    lime wedges, to serve

1 Stir the rhubarb, ginger, sugar and
   200ml (8fl oz) water in a
   saucepan over a medium to high
   heat until the sugar dissolves.
   Bring to the boil and cook for 5–8
   minutes, until thickened slightly.
2 Push through a sieve into a bowl.
   It should give you roughly 500ml
   (16fl oz) of syrup. Leave to cool,
   then chill in the fridge.
3 Fill 8 glasses with ice then divide the
   syrup between each one. Add
   50ml (2fl oz) vodka and 1 teaspoon
   of lime juice to each one. Top with
   ginger beer, stir and garnish with
   mint leaves and lime wedges.

APPLE & ELDERFLOWER MARTINI

MAKES 2

INGREDIENTS
75ml (3fl oz) vodka
25ml (1fl oz) sweet
    vermouth
50ml (2fl oz) cloudy apple
    juice
25ml (1fl oz) elderflower
    cordial
15ml (½fl oz) lime juice
slices of apple, to garnish

Mix everything together in a cocktail
shaker filled with ice. Strain and pour
into a chilled martini glass, then
garnish with a slice of apple.

BATIDA DE COCO

MAKES 1

INGREDIENTS
120ml (4fl oz) coconut
  milk
60ml (2fl oz) cachaça
ice cubes
2 tbsp condensed milk

Easy, really! Simply whizz all the ingredients together in a blender, pour and serve!

You can garnish it with toasted coconut flakes if you want to make it look a bit fancy . . .

POMEGRANATE & CLEMENTINE BELLINI

MAKES 1

INGREDIENTS
50ml (2fl oz) clementine
  juice
150ml (5fl oz) prosecco
  or champagne
10ml (½fl oz) grenadine
25g (1oz) pomegranate
  seeds

Pour the clementine juice into a flute and top with your choice of bubbles. Garnish with the grenadine (it is a heavier liquid so will sink to the bottom of the glass) and a few pomegranate seeds.

INDEX

First published in 2014 by
Deborah McKenna Ltd
64-66 Glentham Road
London, SW13 9JJ

About Autogrill/HMSHost
Autogrill is the world's leading provider of food and beverage services for people on the move. Active in 30 countries and with over 56,000 employees, it has 4,700 points of sale in more than 1,000 locations and operates concession agreements in airports, motorways and railway stations, as well as in selected shopping centres, trade fairs and cultural sites. The company has a portfolio of over 250 international and local brands, managed directly or under license. Listed on the Milan stock exchange, Autogrill is indirectly controlled by Edizione S.r.l., the financial arm of the Benetton family, with 50.1% of the share capital.

Deborah McKenna Ltd supports the Forest Stewardship Council® (FSC®), the leading international forest-certification organisation. Our books carrying the FSC label are printed on FSC®-certified paper. FSC is the only forest-certification scheme supported by the leading environmental organisations, including Greenpeace.

Design and production: XAB Design
Food photography: Georgia Glynn Smith
Portrait photography: Ruth Jenkinson

Printed and bound in Italy by L.E.G.O. S.p.A

ISBN 978-0-9929232-0-4

THANK YOU!

We've had great fun putting this book together and it wouldn't have been possible without all the hard work and dedication from a huge team of fantastic people. We would like to say a massive thanks to Autogrill, Heathrow, Borra Garson and all at Deborah McKenna Ltd, Nigel Wright and XAB Design, Laura Herring, photographers Georgia Glynn Smith and Ruth Jenkinson and their assistants. Gia Mills, Ellie Jarvis, Bacchus PR, Belgraves Hotel and all our fabulous chefs and restaurant team at The Gorgeous Kitchen, Heathrow Terminal 2. Thank you, thank you all!